The Three Faces of Literary Criticism

By Xu Hongjun

Translated by Sun Suning（孙苏宁）

CHICAGO ACADEMIC PRESS

The Three Faces of Literary Criticism
Author: Xu Hongjun
Translator: Sun Suning（孙苏宁）
Language: English
Word Count (for space of all pages): Approximately 196,000 words
Publisher: Chicago Academic Press
Number of Pages: 226
ISBN 978-1-965890-93-6

Publishing	Chicago Academic Press
	5923 N Artesian Ave
	Chicago IL 60659
Email	contact@chicagoacademicpress.com
Website	http://chicagoacademicpress.com/
Book Size	6X9 inches
First Edition	November, 2025

CONTENT

Series I Contemporary Literary Criticism in Henan 1

Revision of Versions and Writing of Trauma 3

1. Contents of the Revision 3

2. The significance of the revisions 9

3. The Value of Traumatic Memory Writing 14

Tian Zhonghe's Literary Chronicle 22

The "Fading" Countryside and the "Blurred" City - A Side of Henan Short Stories and Novellas in 2017 55

I. The Distortion of Experience and the "Fading" of the Countryside 56

II. Women's growth and the absence of the city 65

Torturing Humanity with Feminism, or the Other Way Around 75

I. The Approaching Torture of Human Nature 76

II. The Organization of the Narrative Structure 84

III. The Meticulous Details of the Novel 86

IV. The Psychological Depiction of the Novel 89

Series II Literary Studies of the 1980s 93

Categorizing Writers' Memoirs of the 1980s - Taking New Literary Historical Materials as the Center 95

I. Autobiographical Texts 96

II. Writings on commemoration of writers 103

III. Memories of Literary Societies, Literary Movements, Literary Newspapers and Publications, or Important Literary Historical Facts 111

The Significance, Present Situation and Possibilities of Research on Memoirs of Writers in the 1980s 118

I. Reconstructing the Literary History of the 1980s: The Significance of the Study 118

II. the seriously neglected literary historical facts: the current situation of the research 121

III. Definition of concepts - Organization of historical materials - Textual analysis – Historical Construction: the rationale of the research 126

The Meaning of Historicization and Its Possibilities 140

I. Defining the Concept of "Historicization of Contemporary Literature" 140

II. The Controversial Focus of "Historicization of Contemporary Literature" 145

III. "Historicization of Contemporary Literature" and Related Work 149

Serie III New Century Literary Criticism 163

The Extreme Flower: Telling a Different Story after *Blind Mountain* 165

Unconscious Divergence, Dislocation and Annihilation 175

I. Internal Disagreements among the Constructors of "New Century Literature" 177

II. The dislocation of criticism and the annihilation of academics 189

A Long Way to Go 195

Afterwords 217

Series I Contemporary Literary Criticism in Henan

Revision of Versions and Writing of Trauma

- From *Liang Guangzheng's Glorious Dream to Liang Guangzheng's Light*

In 2017, Liang Hong, a young writer who is known for his non-fiction writing, published his first full-length novel, *Liang Guangzheng's Dream of Glory*, in Issue 5 of Contemporary, and in November 2017, the novel, which was substantially revised and titled *Liang Guangzheng's Light*, was released by the People's Literature Publishing House. "From the early 1950s to the mid-1970s, it was mainly the changes in the political situation and the corresponding changes in literary concepts that led to the emergence of new editions of the work." "From the end of the 1970s to the present, the emergence of new editions of contemporary literature is mainly due to the motivation of artistic perfection."[1]. So, in the face of Liang Hong's revising behavior, we cannot help but ask: why did the writer revise her work so eagerly when it was just published? What did she revise? What is the change between the revised version and the first published version?

How to understand this change? These questions involve not only our analysis of the writer's creative psychology, but also our understanding and evaluation of the novel.

1. Contents of the Revision

Through a detailed comparison of the Contemporary version and the one-volume version, we found that Liang Hong revised the work in five main aspects.

The first is the change of narrative point of view. Except for the last chapter, the *Contemporary* adopts the first-person protagonist narrative point of view. Only the narrator has changed, Liang Dongyu is the narrator of the

1 Jin Hongyu, "Versions of Contemporary Literature", Guangming Daily, February 4, 2004.

second, fifth and eighth chapters, while Liang Dongzhu is the narrator of the first, third, fourth, sixth, seventh and ninth chapters. In fact, from the content of the story and the portrayal of the characters, we can't see any significant difference between Liang Dongyu and Liang Dongzhu. [1]This can also be verified in the revision of the novel. There are several places where the character of the story in the Contemporary version is Liang Dongzhu or Liang Dongyu, but it is changed to Liang Dongyu or Liang Dongzhu in the stand-alone version. From this detail, we may be able to see that Liang Dongzhu and Liang Dongyu are actually the same person. Therefore, basically we can think that the narrative point of view of the *Contemporary* is the first-person protagonist narrative point of view.

The single-volume narrative perspective, however, is omniscient. The narrative personal pronoun "I" has been changed to "冬竹（Dong Zhu）" or "冬玉（Dong Yu）". This is not a problem in most places, but in some places, it still makes people feel awkward. For example, "father", if this title follows a character in the novel, we think it is not a big problem; we will naturally imagine him as the father of Dongzhu and Dongyu, but throughout the whole book, except for Chapter 10, Liang Guangzheng appeared with the title "father". But throughout the book, except for Chapter 10, Liang Guangzheng is addressed as "father", who is addressing him in this way? It can only be one of his children, and all his children are placed in the story of the novel under their own names, so they cannot stand apart from the scene of their own stories and call themselves "father" from the standpoint of a narrator. Therefore, in the single book, this name is actually very awkward. Similarly, there is the case of "we". In the one-volume version, we no longer see the narrator "I" on the surface. However, a plural personal pronoun "we"

1 For example, Liang Guangzheng's Light, People's Literature Publishing House, 2017 edition, pp. 163, 178, 207, 236, corresponds to the Contemporary edition, pp. 62, 61, 70, 78 respectively.

exists everywhere in the novel. In the story, this "we" refers to the four sisters, Dongxue, Dongzhu, Yongzhi, and Dongyu, and the "I" in "we" should be one of the four siblings, and they all exist in the novel as characters. All of them exist in the novel as story characters, so who is this "I" who calls "we"? He is obviously not the God-like narrator in the omniscient point of view, nor is he an innovation of the author in the narrative point of view. Frankly speaking, he is only a remnant of the first-person narrative point of view that has not been completely transformed by the author during the revision process. Therefore, even in the one-volume book, the first-person narrative protagonist has not completely withdrawn, he is still in control of the rhythm of the story, overlooking the development of the story from above, and experiencing the sorrows and joys of the characters.

The second element of the revision is the interregnum part in the *Contemporary* and the epigraph has been deleted or adapted to the main text of the novel.

These changes are actually brought about by the change of narrative perspective. Since *Contemporary* is originally a first-person protagonist narrative perspective, it is logically impossible for the narrator to know everything about the other characters. In the novel, if she wants to tell her other characters, she needs to use external forces, and the interregnum and epigraph play just such a role. "I am like a detective, surrounded by piles of letters, diaries, scraps of paper, and all sorts of clutter. One by one, I examine them—each letter, each diary, each fragment—piecing together time, plot, story, and hidden secrets."[1]With the narrative background of interregnum and epigraph, all the narratives of "I" to other characters become real and believable.

1 Liang Hong: "Liang Guangzheng's Glorious Dream", Contemporary, Issue 5, 2017, p. 5.

Because of the change of the narrative perspective of the novel, the interregnum and the epigraph became a burden, and had to be deleted.

In the third case of revision, two types of contents in *Contemporary* have been deleted from the main text of the single-volume version. One is the text that has little to do with the main content. For example, at the beginning of the third chapter, there were three paragraphs describing the Rang County Bridge in *Contemporary*, but the story behind had little to do with them, so the single-volume edition directly deleted all of them. There are many other similar cases. Through this kind of deletion, the main story of the novel becomes cleaner, more compact and clearer. Another type of content deleted is text with a strong lyrical quality. Some contents can only be told by the first-person narrator; if replaced by the third person, it will be obviously inappropriate to tell such words.

In order to maintain the harmony between the narrative perspective and the narrative tone, almost all of these elements have been deleted. For example, there is a sentence on page 25 in *Contemporary*: “I can’t stand the thought of seeing that woman again, I can’t stand the thought of seeing that child, I don’t want to go back to the past.” In the single-volume edition, the narrator of this chapter, “I”, is replaced by Dongzhu. In this narrative perspective, if the above sentence is changed to: “Dongzhu can’t bear to see that woman again, Dongzhu can’t bear to see that child, she doesn’t want to go back to the past.” It is very unnatural to read.

However, the deletion of some parts was not successful. For example, in Chapter 4, before the fight in Guangzhou, the *Contemporary* originally contained a paragraph that began, “Yung-chi never realized how he was dragged into the fight.” [1] Then it goes on to summarize his frequent fights at

1 Liang Hong, “Liang Guangzheng’s Glorious Dream”, Contemporary, No. 5, 2017, p. 46.

Wuzhen High School. With this recollection, the subsequent account of the fight in Guangzhou would not be out of place, and it could also foreshadow the severity of the fight in Guangzhou. With this memory cut from the single-volume, the plot of the fight in Guangzhou would appear to be abrupt and incoherent.

The fourth case of revision is the addition of a considerable amount of text to the body of the text in the one-volume version. From the point of view of narrative effect, the added words are mainly to make the narrative tighter and the plot more coherent. For example, in the second chapter, before Liang Guangzheng took Manzi to work as a migrant worker Barbara had a fierce conflict with Yongzhi. The *Contemporary* is more ambiguous about the details of this conflict, describing only that Liang Guangzheng was attacked by a brute girl.

He was so angry that "his body was trembling" and "his veins were jumping up and down"; Yongzhi eagerly argued, "No, no, I didn't"; the brute girl indignantly questioned, "You didn't? You didn't?" We do not know exactly what happened. The single-volume version of the incident on pages 53-54 makes a necessary supplement. Through this supplement, we generally know the original story, the brute girl was suspected of Yongzhi peeping at her, and told this to Liang Guangzheng, which led to the accusation, defense and persuasion between the three people.

The fifth scenario of revision is similar to the fourth one, and its intention is mainly to make the narrative of the novel smoother and more natural, and more in line with the logic of the development of the story. However, the way of revision is not to delete or add, but to adjust the narrative structure. There are two ways to do so. One is to adjust the order of the narrative content. For example, in the last two paragraphs of Chapter 1, the order in the *Contemporary* edition is "the Spring Festival the year after Mom's death" and "one year ago". In the single-volume edition, the order was adjusted to "the year before Mom's death" and "the spring of the year after Mom's death". As far as the internal logic of the story is concerned, it is clear that the one-volume version makes more sense. This kind of sequence adjustment occurs most frequently in Chapter 6, with nine adjustments to the order of larger passages.[1] For example, Liang Guangzheng's two letters to Dongxue were originally placed at the beginning of this chapter in the *Contemporary* version, which appeared to be very abrupt;

The single-volume version puts them in the middle of the paragraphs describing Liang Guangzheng's relationship with his children, which on the one hand can be used as evidence of Liang Guangzheng's sincere feelings for his children, and on the other hand seems to be more fluent and natural. Another way of reordering seems to occur more frequently in the one-volume version. It is to divide the large narrative in the *Contemporary* text into smaller paragraphs according to the main meaning of the text. The greatest advantage of this restructuring of the text is that it makes the textual space of the novel appear more spacious and easier to read. For example, in Chapter 2, after the bumper harvest of Liang Zhuang's maitong, the Guangzhou men delayed in purchasing it, and everyone was very anxious and gathered around Liang Guangzheng to discuss the matter. This paragraph, page 21 of the *Contemporary*, was originally two very dense dialogues, without a colon and quotation marks in the middle, it is a bit difficult to read. In the single-volume edition, page 46 was reformatted into multiple dialogue paragraphs, complete

---

1 From this, we can also see that in this chapter, the author was deeply immersed in the writing of traumatic memories. In China in Liangzhuang and in several different editions of interviews, Liang Hong repeatedly talks about her mother and the profound impact of her mother's constant bed-riddenness on her childhood memories. When the writer is immersed in the writing of such traumatic memories, she may not be able to take into account the logic of the narrative at all. She can (and should) only follow her memories and express her feelings as they come to her. Only in this way will she be able to bring out the most distant memories of her deepest heart, and to release the deep emotions that have been suppressed for years.

with colons and quotation marks, which makes the text much clearer and easier to read. \\

From the comparison of the above five aspects, we can find that the scale of revision of this novel is very large: from the narrative perspective to the narrative structure, from the narrative content to the textual space, all of them have undergone great changes. The impact of such changes on the work should not be ignored, and the author's creative mind behind such a large-scale revision in such a short time is also worth paying attention to.

2. The significance of the revisions

From the last three revisions, it can be seen that the author's revision is mainly out of consideration of text structure and the reader's acceptance.

The narrative style of the *Contemporary* satisfies the author's need to write memories and express emotions. When the author is immersed in her own memory space and emotional world, her creativity enters a state of madness, she follows the flow of her memory and emotion, and in this artistic world she sees her childhood and her hometown. These situations and fragments of memory sprang up in her mind like a spring, and she did not have time to sort them out, to recognize them, or to arrange their positions. She treasures this feeling of creation so much that she can't bear to interrupt it, can't afford to miss it, and simply lets them "automatically" spread out in the text of the novel. This kind of unrestrained creative experience has brought unprecedented pleasure to the author, but it has also brought some intolerable problems to the novel itself: some of its contents do not conform to the logic of facts, and many of its paragraphs are too long, so that the readers can't make sense of the clues of the story on the one hand, and they can't catch their breath because of the big paragraphs of the narration on the other hand. This state of the text is, in any case, intolerable for both the author and the reader. It was inevitable that the author would revise it.

The reason for the author's revision of the first two scenarios is probably the desire to keep the narrative style as objective, cool, restrained, and subdued as possible. The First-Person narrative perspective has one feature: it facilitates the narrator to tell a story about himself and his own acquaintance and to express his subjective feelings in the course of the narrative. However, it also has its own limitations, as it tends to make the narrative too subjective and uncontrolled, and to make the reader equate the narrator with the writer. Both of these are what Hong tried to avoid in the process of revision. An overly subjective and uncontrolled narration will easily lead to the confusion of narrative logic and too rapid narrative rhythm, which will make readers feel depressed and rejected in the process of reading, and this is something that should be avoided as much as possible in the process of disseminating a novel. It is also necessary to avoid equating the narrator with the author, especially when it comes to his family history and personal privacy. This is also evident in the revision of the novel.

The novel has a very strong autobiographical color. This is not only reflected in the narrative perspective, but also in the content of the novel and some detailed issues. As far as the content is concerned, Liang Guangzheng, Mai's daughter, Yongzhi, Dongxue, and the stories that happened to them in the novel have been dealt with to varying degrees in Liang Hong's previous non-fictional books *China in Liangzhuang*, *The Record of Going Out of Liangzhuang*, and the interview *Liangzhuang: The Present and Future of Rural China - An Interview with Liang Hong*. The names Liang Guangzheng and Mai Daughter are probably fictitious, but the stories that happened to them have been preserved from *China in Liangzhuang* to *Liang Guangzheng's Light*: the father who fought against oppression, pursued justice, did not love labor, and loved to fight injustice, the mother who was afraid for her husband in her early years and was bedridden in her later years. these two characters maintain a striking consistency in these two works of different genres. The nature of Yongzhi 's work and love experience also reminds us of the "ideal young man who left his hometown" in *China in Liangzhuang*. The character and experience of Dongxue, the "elder sister", is also quite similar to the "elder sister" mentioned by Liang Hong in his interview: "My elder sister is the pillar of my sisters.

She was even more important than my father."[1] The description of the character Dongxue "riding a bicycle" in the interregnum part of *Contemporary*, "wanting to ride down the road", also resembles the scene of the interview with the older sister riding a bicycle after a breakup: "My sister told me the other day that when the boy told her he was breaking up with her, she rode her bicycle on the street as if she were lost, but she didn't know where she was riding to."[2] As a fictional text, the similarities between the novel, its characters, its story and the non-fictional text cannot help but make people think of the autobiographical color of the novel.

Narrative content of these documentary features already let us on its autobiographical color to the imagination, if we add the first person protagonist narrative perspective and emphasis on the diary, letters and other "real" information, we can simply determine that the novel of Dongzhu, Dongyu is Liang Hong, Liang Guangzheng's family story is a replica of the story of Liang Hong's family. This is obviously what the writer does not want to see. Therefore, in the single-volume book, the narrative perspective was changed to a more "objective" omniscient perspective. The "Interregnum" and "Inscription", which can be easily associated, have also been removed or transformed and integrated into the content of the main text.

---

1 Liang Hong and Zhang Lijun, "Liang Zhuang: The Present and Future of Rural China - An Interview with Liang Hong", Hundred Years of Review, No. 2, 2015, pp. 44-45.
2 ② Liang Hong and Zhang Lijun, "Liang Zhuang: The Present and Future of Lushaigo China - Liang Hong's Interviews", Hundred Schools Review, Vol. 2, No. 2, 2015, p. 45.

Based on the above two analyses, we can generally think that Liang Hong's revision is basically a success: the logic of the narrative is more coherent and reasonable, the content of the story is clearer and more concise, the space of the text is more sparse, and the expression of the novel is more objective and neutral. In Liang Hong's mind, it may be more like a novel.

But the question does not end there.Because an obvious question lies before us: if there was so much dissatisfaction with the original version, why was it published in the first place? Why didn't they wait for the revisions to be published? What is the value of the *Contemporary* version compared to the single-volume version? Does it have something that a single volume cannot replace? These questions are perhaps more interesting than the previous ones.

The first thing we need to recognize is that even after the revision, *Contemporary* still has its value. This value is on the one hand for the writers themselves and on the other hand related to our study of the writers. Writers as creators are different from writers as readers. After the release of *Liang Guangzheng's Glorious Dream*, Liang Hong, as a reader, can naturally perceive the problems that exist in the novel. However, Liang Hong, as a reader, cannot stand in for the Liang Hong who created it. For Liang Hong as the subject of creation, the problems that she found while reading may be the precious experience that she cherished while creating. In the creation of *Liang Guangzheng's Glorious Dream*, Liang Hong integrated her life memories into the novel, into the characters, and through the construction of the novel's world and imagination, she wrote the life memories that had been suppressed in her heart for a long time. It is precisely because writes soundly and without fear about the memories of life that the novel does not hesitate to adopt the first-person protagonist narrative perspective at the beginning, because only this perspective can fully write the memories that she has buried in her heart for a long time, and only such a perspective allows her to freely express her deep feelings, and at any time comment on the personnel in the novel. It is also because of this kind of completely devoted life memory writing that she has no time to pay attention to the first-person narrative, for only such a perspective can adequately capture her long-held, buried memories. Furthermore, it's the only viewpoint enabling her to freely articulate her profound affections and readily offer observations on the people and occurrences within the novel.

It's precisely this fully immersed writing of life memories that led her to disregard the novel's narrative logic, story content, textual space, and narrative style. Instead, she primarily wrote freely, guided by the flow of her own memories and emotions. Only by understanding this can we understand why there are irrationalities in the narrative logic of *Contemporary*, why there are so many changes in the story, why the text of the novel is often so large and unparagraphed, and why the style of the text is so eager and direct. All of this is because the creative subject immersed in the writing of life memories can no longer take these technical matters into account. Therefore, the author's publication of *Liang Guangzheng's Glorious Dream* before the revision is not only not an impulse, but also should be understood as a kind of respect for sincere creation and text retention. It is precisely because the author has preserved such an original text which is "subject to revision" that we have the possibility of exploring the traumatic memory writing of this novel. In this sense, we believe that the revision has both gains and losses. In terms of success, it has made the narrative logic of the novel more rigorous, the story content smoother, the text more sparse, the narrative style calmer, and has also weakened the autobiographical color of the novel to a certain extent. But it is a little regrettable that, if not read the single-volume edition with the *Contemporary*, this revision may form a shield to that valuable experience of traumatic memories writing, and this point is an important focus on the study of the writer's state of mind during the writing creation.

3. The Value of Traumatic Memory Writing

This novel, especially the *Contemporary* version, can be regarded as a typical text of traumatic memory writing. This kind of writing is mainly reflected in the novel in the following aspects: narrative perspective, narrative structure, narrative content, narrative style, the creation of human figures and the description of the novel's scenes.

Essentially, the narrative perspective of the novel is omniscient, but in the contemporary version, the author also makes the characters in the novel act as first-person narrators, telling their own stories or learning about others' stories through diary entries. Since the function of the narrative requires the narrator to take on God's role, why not use the third-person narrative perspective directly, as in the revised single-volume version? It can be seen that the omniscient narrative perspective did not fulfill certain needs of the author when he started to write.

This need comes from a distant voice deep in the author's heart: she needs to express freely the traumatic memories that have been suppressed in her heart. From the perspective of telling her inner trauma, the first-person protagonist narrative perspective is undoubtedly the most appropriate, which is more conducive to the narrator's telling of her inner trauma. The prerequisite for getting rid of traumatic memories is the narration and construction of trauma. "Cultural trauma is not a self-experiential fact, but a conscious cultural construction, with consciousness, subjectivity and reflectivity,

It is a specific writing representation of the facts of experience.[1]In this sense, the best way for the narrator to overcome his traumatic memory is to tell his inner trauma either by himself or in his own face. In this regard, the revision of this novel may be regarded as a ritual or celebration given by the

1 Tao Dongfeng, Cultural Trauma and Witness Literature, Contemporary Literature Forum, No. 5, 2011.

author after the completion of the trauma narrative: "The ritual act, as a symbolic demonstration of action, is a manifestation of the unique symbolic capacity of human beings. Literature, as a symbolic linguistic expression, can certainly be regarded as a linguistic extension of the ritual performance, and is thus also characterized by fiction and demonstration." [1]

In *Contemporary*, the narrative structure of this novel appears in a state of vacancy, repetition, inversion and disorganization: is this a narrative strategy or a special manifestation of the author's traumatic memory writing? In the novel, there is this sentence: "I just want to put together the past days, I want to put together a diagram, to see how the shape, the trend and the logic of development of that diagram have become what it is today." [2]This perhaps reveals the fact that the author is trying to put together the past, the past, the present, and the future. This may reveal a message that the narrator wishes to tell a story with internal logic, but, as seen in *Contemporary*, this wish is not fully realized at the beginning, and some of the stories seem to be too abrupt in their succession, lacking some necessary logical relationships in the middle. In our opinion, this does not seem to be an intentional narrative strategy as in pioneering literature, but a special manifestation of the author's traumatic memory writing. "Narrative is a framework, according to which human beings assign meaning to temporal experiences and experiences of personal action."

"Narrative provides a framework for understanding the past and for envisioning the future. It is a major framework within which human existence

1 Ye Shuxian edited Literature and Therapy (updated edition), Shaanxi Normal University Press, 2018, p. 301.
2 Liang Hong, "Liang Guangzheng's Glorious Dream", Contemporary, No. 5, 2017, p. 65.

is made meaningful."[1] In this sense, when there are still some logical gaps within a narrative framework, perhaps the narrator has not yet fully emerged from his inner traumatic memories. Therefore, we can also say that the revision of the novel is not only a literary act, but also a psychological one. In the literary sense, it further enhances the literary quality of the novel; and from the point of view of traumatic memory healing, it may also mean that through the writing of traumatic memories in the *Contemporary*, the subject of the novel has, to a certain extent, come out of the shadow of traumatic memories in his own heart.

In terms of recollections, the teenage years of the four children of the Liang family were almost entirely characterized by exhausting trauma. Three of the most important are: the nosy father, the mother's bedridden, and the serious burns of Xiao Feng. The nosy father brought "us" more than the image and pride of "heroes", but the constant worry and fear. Our sick mother brings us more "hurt" and "disgust" than sympathy and pity: "Mom is naked, like a skeleton, ugly, and she looks like a woman. Mom was naked, like a skeleton, an ugly, dirty, disliked skeleton, like a rag, at the mercy of others." [2]"At a very young age, I had seen Mom's most private parts countless times, and they were out in the open.

It's ugly, so ugly. I really don't like it. I feel like I've been hurt. I'm sick of seeing bodies. I hate seeing each other's bodies."[3] Even when "I" was teased by my classmates for having lice on my head, "I" thought, "It's all because I don't have a mom. I called out to my mom, mom, but she didn't

1 Polkinghorne: Narrative knowing and the human sciences, cited in Li Ming, Yang Guangxue: Introduction to Narrative Psychotherapy, Shandong People's Publishing House,2005,p.52.

2 Liang Hong: Liang Guangzheng's Glorious Dream, Contemporary, No. 5, 2017, p. 61.

3 Liang Hong: "Liang Guangzheng's Glorious Dream", Contemporary, No. 5, 2017, p. 61.

answer me"[1]. Worse still, Xiao Feng's burns, because it may involve "our" responsibility, so, for "us", it is a gradually growing "tumor", one day it spills out its poison. One day the venom it spills out will "drown" us, "corrode" us. No one wants to mention it, even in the narrative, "we" will intentionally isolate it. "We" are like this, not because "we" have forgotten, but because "we don't know where to start. It's too heavy and too deep. It is a black hole that once opened, you will be sucked in and never be able to climb out, never to see the sun and the light again."③[2] The writing of such a heavy, traumatic memory brings readers a heart-rending reading experience, and it is even more of a heart-rending psychological experience in the author's creative process.

What also characterizes this novel of traumatic memory writing is its narrative style." Style is the expressive form of language, which is partly determined by the psychological characteristics of the performer and partly by the content and intention of the performance."[3] In *Contemporary*, the narrative style of this novel is highlighted as a personal and lyrical style.

The narrative style of the novel derives from the first-person narrative perspective on the one hand, and the narrative content of the novel on the other. According to the above discussion, thc first person's narrative perspective is greatly influenced by the author's traumatic memory writing, and the content of these personalized narratives is often closely related to the author's traumatic memory writing. For example, on *Contemporary*, p.17, "I have vague memories of the horrors of those years at home". P.49, "I remember the screams, I remember the cries, I remember the eyes that looked at me

---

1 Liang Hong: "Liang Guangzheng's Glorious Dream", Contemporary, Issue 5, 2017, p. 95.

2 Liang Hong: Liang Guangzheng's Glorious Dream, Contemporary, Issue 5, 2017, p. 59.

3 Wicknagel, Goethe, Coleridge, etc.: A Theory of Literary Style, translated by Wang Yuanhua, Shanghai Translation and Literature Publishing House, 1982, p. 18.

when he left, black and bright, I always remember them, they clamored in my head all night long, like grain seeds, planted and sprouting all the time. For so many years, I have been trying my best to forget it, trying my best to press it down, letting it wither and extinguish until it dies". The lyricism in the narrative style of this novel is also very obvious. For example, on *Contemporary*, p.28, there is a direct appeal by the narrator, Dongzhu: "O Lord, have mercy on us, have mercy on us. For we have been despised to the uttermost. We are despised to the uttermost by the scorn of the comfortable, and by the contempt of the proud." This kind of intensely personal lyricism is found in many other places in the novel, and they are often found in passages written about traumatic memories. So, fundamentally speaking, traumatic memory writing has a profound influence on the narrative style of the novel.

Traumatic memory writing also affects the characterization of the novel. Liang Guangzheng, on the surface, "he is a saint, he is Q, he is a fool, he is a dreamer, he is a father, he is a land, he is a naughty child, he is a destroyer"[1].

But in the depths of his heart, however, there was a deep-seated fear and trauma, which he did not want to show in front of the children. When he was young, he was criticized and hunted down for his pursuit of justice and righteousness, and later he was beaten half to death by his in-laws for being a barbarian. When he was in a state of hallucination in his life, he had revealed the depths of his inner world: "Don't hit me, don't hit me, I still have four children at home, and the children's mother, lying in bed, I can't move, I have to go back, I have to go back ah, you beat me to death, they all have to die, don't hit, don't hit."[2] These traumas suffered in his youth he did not tell anyone, but on the surface he was still so "troublesome", so stubborn, so

1 This is the evaluation of the character of Liang Guangzheng by the famous literary critic Mr. Li Jingze. See The Light of Liang Guangzheng, People's Literature Publishing House, back cover of 2017 edition.
2 Liang Hong, "Liang Guangzheng's Glorious Dream", Contemporary, No. 5, 2017, p. 80.

unreasonable. These traumas suffered in his youth he did not tell anyone, on the surface is still so "trouble", so stubborn, so unreasonable, but this is not the complete Liang Guangzheng. A complete Liang Guangzheng not only pursues fairness and justice, loves to meddle in affairs, aspires to love, is passionate about women, is tired of land, is full of ideals, and has achieved nothing despite repeated trials and tribulations, but also is full of trauma and fear deep down in his heart, longing for his mother's breasts and arms, and yearning for safety and warmth. Liang Guangcheng is full and complex, not only the "light" floating on the surface of his life, but also the "wounds" deep in his bones. Not only "his children have never really entered his world"[1], but it also takes time and life experience for us to enter his heart.

Liang Hong's ability to portray psychology and describe scenes is astonishing. For example, in this paragraph, "Twenty years have passed, the whole family seems to have conspired, coincidentally forgot the barbarian, no one mentioned her name, including Dong Yu, who was only twelve years old at the time.

Everyone automatically skipped the chapter on the brute girl, as if there had never been a brute girl and nothing had ever happened. When it comes to those years, we don't even have the insight to look at each other, so we automatically cut out the scene about the brute girl. But how can it be deleted? If the process of life can be shown in photographs, then the photographs of our family must have been fragmented and shapeless in those years, and all our lives were changed by the arrival of brute girl, but we insisted on refusing to show her color and her position, so the photographs looked like they had been infested by worms, washed by water, and ground by sand, and there was always a blurred, black-hole-like avatar standing there, facing the people who looked at it. No one wants to look at it, but everyone knows that it has always

1 This is Liang Hong's evaluation of Liang Guangzheng in a media interview.

been there, hibernating in the deepest recesses of memory, waiting for an opportunity to come back at us"[1]. This kind of ability to draw a psychological picture and lay out a scenario can never be achieved by an unprepared writer. How could a writer have such an outstanding ability to portray? On this point, Liang Hong once said in an interview: "For me, childhood may be a very closed environment...... This has accidentally given me a space that I can't describe, a space for free meditation. This kind of space encourages you to explore more about the natural world, about your inner self, which is fortunate in hindsight, and allows you to have more detailed thoughts."[2] A closed childhood with traumatic memories nurtured Liang Hong's ability to meticulously observe both the external environment and the inner world. Coupled with the writing habits developed since his youth, it is easy to understand that Liang Hong showed special abilities in psychological and situational descriptions as soon as he started to write.

From *Liang Guangzheng's Glorious Dream* to *Liang Guangzheng's Light*, from the creation of the novel, its publication to its subsequent revision and publication, as well as the creative mentality of the writer and the motivation of revision reflected in the process, all should be regarded as a whole united text. The reading of this "united text" is far more meaningful than analyzing a single version of it. This "united text" not only reflects the valuable experience of sound and full devotion in the writer's initial creative process, but also presents the various problems brought by this creative mindset to the novel itself. It not only reflects the respect and cherishing for the initial creative mind of the writer as the creative subject, but also shows the excellence of the writer as the reader in the pursuit of the artistic aesthetics of his work.

---

1 Liang Hong, "Liang Guangzheng's Glorious Dream", Contemporary, No. 5, 2017, p. 13.

2 Liang Hong and Zhang Lijun, "Liang Zhuang: The Present and Future of Rural China - Liang Hong's Interviews", Hundred Years of Review, Issue 2, 2015.

It not only reflects the whole process of writing trauma memories, but also the rituals and celebrations that the writer brings to himself after the completion of trauma memory writing. Therefore, this “united text” has a typical literary value, whether it is to analyze the aesthetic color and artistic value of the novel itself, or to explore the writer’s mentality and the process of creating.

Tian Zhonghe's Literary Chronicle[1]

1941, one year old

Tian Zhonghe, formerly known as Zhang Qihua, was born on February 5, 1941 (the tenth day of the first month of the Xin Si year on the lunar calendar)[2] to a small merchant family in Pai Fang Street, Tanghe County, Henan Province, and his ancestral home was a foreign-accented camp (Dazhuangzhuang) under the Wenfeng Pagoda, three miles east of the city. Tian Zhonghe's great-grandfather[3]

Zhang Fengwu was the last xiucai to pass the prefectural examination in Tanghe County. On this point, Tian Zhonghe mentioned it more than once in his autobiographical novels such as *Seventeen*, but it seems that this literary lineage, which he could be proud of, was not inherited from Tian Zhonghe's father.

"I have always felt that I am a lucky man. God has made me in a small county with a long history, born in a family of small merchants who are neither rich nor poor, and given me a wise and strong mother and two brothers

---

1 In the process of compiling the chronicle, Mr. Tian Zhonghe provided a lot of first-hand information for the author, and reviewed and revised the chronicle five times. Special thanks to him.

2 The date is confirmed by the author to Mr. Tian Zhonghe himself. In some official introductions and curriculum vitae, the date of birth of Mr. Tian Zhonghe is shown as Dec. 15, 1941, according to the introduction of Mr. Tian Zhonghe. According to Tian Zhonghe, the error was caused by the carelessness of the two young staff members who counted the household registration in those years. When Tian Zhonghe discovered the error and asked for a change, he realized that it was not as easy as he had imagined to change the information in his household. Because it is not a particularly important error, Tian Zhonghe simply put the error on the wrong, and has been used.

3 In the work Grandfather's Coffin and Grandmother's Donkey, Tian Zhonghe uses the word "old master", where the word "爷" is not pronounced softly, and 老爷 (lǎoyé) means great-grandfather. In the 2011 edition of Seventeen by Jiangsu Literary Publishing House, "老爷" is mistakenly changed to "姥爷" (Tian Zhonghe, Seventeen, Jiangsu Literary Publishing House, 2011, p. 23). The word "grand-mother" is the name of a maternal grandfather, which is not at all the same thing as "old-master" in the Henan dialect.

with literary talent and romantic temperament."[1] "There are many stories in small towns, and the county town is a place where rural and urban cultures meet, and it is a very good stage for the performance of human nature. Born in a family of small businessmen, I grew up behind the counter, watching the behavior of people coming and going, and listening to all kinds of legends and stories in the marketplace. Many of my novels come from my mother's stories, from the memories of my neighbors and shopkeepers in my childhood. My hometown county gave me rich literary resources." [2]

Tanghe County, located in the southwest of Henan Province and bordering Hubei Province, has a long civilization history and rich cultural deposits, producing many historical and cultural celebrities such as the famous philosopher Feng Youlan, the geologist Feng Jinglan, the writer Feng Yuanjun, the writer Zong Pu, the poet Li Ji, etc. The traditional folk culture arts such as Han Opera, Qu Opera, Yu Opera, Yue Opera, Drums, etc., which are active in the county have given Tian Zhonghe rich cultural nourishment and artistic inculcation.

1943, at the age of three[3]

My eldest sister, Zhang Shugui, has passed away. At the time of her death, she was a seventeen-year-old[4], a talented student at a girls' school

---

1 Tian Zhonghe: "Literature and happiness - 'Tomorrow's Sun', in Tomorrow's Sun, Henan People's Publishing House, 2014, page 1.
2 Miao Meiling and Tian Zhonghe, "Walking Freely in the Literary Scene: An Interview with Tian Zhonghe", Dongjing Literature, No. 3, 2012.

3 This date was revised by Tian Zhonghe when the author sent the chronicle to him for review. In Seventeen-Year-Old Sister, the author says, "She passed away the year after I was born." (Tian Zhonghe, Seventeen-Year-Old Sister, in A Tree in the Old Garden, Haiyan Publishing House, 2001, pp. 91-92) is incorrect.
4 The age here is in weeks. According to the method of calculating this genealogy, Zhang Shugui was eighteen years old when she died. In many of his works, Tian Zhonghe says that she died at the age of seventeen, so the present genealogy respects the author's statement and does not change it. In addition, when quoting the works of Tian Zhonghe in this chronicle, unless otherwise specified, the age is the weekly age, which is different from the calculation method of this chronicle.

in the prime of her life, with a violent and stubborn character, who died at an early age due to her dissatisfaction with her marriage. The story of the elder sister was written by Tian Zhonghe as a reminiscence essay, *The Seventeen-Year-Old Elder Sister*, which was later incorporated into a full-length novel *Seventeen* under the title *The Seventeen-Year-Old Sister at the Grocery Store.*

Tian Zhonghe's parents had five children: the eldest, Zhang Shugui, was born in 1926 and died at the age of 17. The second daughter, Zhang Shuwen, was born in 1933, the sixth in the line of among her cousins, and was habitually called "sixth sister" by Tian Zhonghe. The second daughter, Zhang Shuwen, born in 1930, was the sixth in line of her cousins, and was customarily called "Sixth Sister" by Tian Zhonghe, whose story of her youth was written by Tian Zhonghe in the novel Sixth Nurse at Seventeen. Zhang Qijun, the eldest son, born in 1931, "was my literary initiator, and he influenced my second brother and me"[1]. His stories mainly appeared in the two chapters of *Seventeen*, "The Young Man's Journey" and "Scabies in the Year of the Rat". Zhang Qirui, the second son, was born in 1934, graduated from Xi'an Jiaotong College, and was one of the first batch of specialized graduates cultivated by the new China.

Because of his love of literature and joining activities in literary activities, he was criticized in the anti-Hu Feng movement, and later classified as a rightist, and sent to the southern border for reform through labor. By the time he was rehabilitated, he was already half a century old and suffered from the paranoia of persecution, unable to integrate into normal society, and soon died of depression. Zhang Qirui had a great influence on Tian Zhonghe; not only did he have an important enlightening effect on his choice of literary

1 Tian Zhonghe: "Literature and Happiness - Prolegomenon to The Sun of Tomorrow", in The Sun of Tomorrow, Henan People's Publishing House, 2014, p. 1.

path, but his rightist status prevented Tian Zhonghe from entering his ideal university, but also his life experiences provided Tian Zhonghe with direct historical experience and emotional experience to reflect on that special era. "Under the influence of the rightist faction of my second brother, I was at a low point in my life and drifted at the bottom of the social ladder. My second brother's books became a spiritual harbor for my wandering career, nourishing and comforting my soul during the difficult years. The red and blue pencil marks left on the book let me touch the heart of my second brother, inspired my desire for literature and respect. My second brother, Chirui, is my literary martyr. He sacrificed himself for literature to fulfill me."[1] In July 1992, Tian Zhonghe wrote *the Monumental Impressions*, a novel that briefly sketched his three marriages, his studies in Xi'an, his work in Xinjiang and the trials and tribulations he suffered, as well as his unfortunate twilight years. In 2015, Tian Zhonghe published another novel, *Kurkala Love*, which was based on his life experiences. His third son, Zhang Qihua, is Tian Zhonghe.

1944, at the age of four

His father, Zhang Fuxiang, died at the age of 59 due to "malaria in the warm season"[2]. Born in 1886[3], Zhang Fuxiang started his business by weaving lanterns and strainers, and opened a grocery store "Fushengchang" in Pai

---

1 Tian Zhonghe, "Blessed by Literature - Prologue to The Sun of Tomorrow", in The Sun of Tomorrow, Henan People's Publishing House, 2014, p. 1.

2 Regarding this disease, Tian Zhonghe had a description, "The mysterious name of the disease that took my father's life, 'malaria in the warm season', was so intimidating that it became an engraved memory in my heart since I was a child. I could never figure out the words of this gray-shaded term, nor could I deduce from which secret codex it came. ... ... When I grew up, I heard my mother say that my father's eyes were yellow when he was dying, and his whole body was covered with yellowish-colored patches, so I wondered if it was acute jaundice hepatitis. If it were really such a clear and definite disease, the sacredness of my father's death would have been diminished, and I would have preferred not to jump to conclusions, and would have preferred that my father had suffered from the mysterious 'malaria in the warm season' that no one understands". Tian Zhonghe. A Tree in the Old Garden, Haiyan Publishing House, 2001, p. 149.

3 According to "Tian Zhonghe's Family Profile" (unpublished) sent to the author by Tian Zhonghe.

Fang Street. At the age of 37, he married his mother, Tian Zhonghe, who was 18 years younger than him.[1] In the late fall of 1944, Zhang Fuxiang suffered a great psychological blow because of the failure of his business and died soon after. "The early death of my father branded my childhood with compassion, making me very sensitive to the world, with sentimentality and sadness becoming the underlying color of my character. Growing up under the pampering of the whole family, I developed an unruly and arrogant personality."[2]

1947, at the age of seven

Enrolled in Tanghe County Private Model Elementary School. The school was the best elementary school of its kind in Tanghe County during the Republic of China. Tian Zhonghe only studied there for half a year before the school was disbanded during the war. Since then, Tian Zhonghe has been wandering around in temporary schools organized by private individuals.

1949, at the age of nine

Tanghe County No.1 Comprehensive Primary School was established, and Tian Zhonghe continued his elementary school education here until he graduated. When he was in the fifth grade of elementary school, he tried to start a long novel with the background that he returned to the county after

---

1 According to the information provided in Jujube and Grain in 1944, Tian Zhonghe and his parents married in 1923, when Zhang Fuxiang was 37 years old. According to Tian Zhonghe's Family Profile, Tian Qin was born in 1903 and should have been 20 years old at the time of her marriage, so Zhang Fuxiang was 17 years older than Tian Qin. But this article says that he was 18 years older. This is a contradiction. In addition, in "Tian Zhonghe Family Profile",Zhang Fuxiang was born in the Year of the Dog, but in this article, it was changed to the Year of the Tiger. . If the article is regarded as a novel, this information is not important; if it is regarded as an autobiographical recollection, such contradictory information should be pointed out.

2 ④Miao Meiling and Tian Zhonghe, "Walking Freely in the Scene of Literature - An Interview with Tian Zhonghe", Dongjing Literature, No. 3, 2012.

fleeing from the disaster and saw his family's yard full of weeds, but he only wrote the beginning with this scene and failed to write the following part.

1953, at the age of thirteen

He was admitted to the junior high school of Tanghe County No.1 Middle School. During this time, Tian Zhonghe was introduced to literature. "The person who led me to literature was my junior high school teacher, Yang Yusen. She came from a famous family and was the first generation of new women in the county. In her language classes, she did not stick to the lesson plan and often read novels to us for several days in a row. She appreciated my writings and used to bring my essays and weekly notes to class to read. With her enthusiastic encouragement, I began to submit articles to magazines until one day, I published my own book."[1]

1956, at the age of sixteen

He was admitted to the senior high school section of Tanghe County No.1 Middle School. During this period, Tian Zhonghe read a lot of Chinese and foreign poems. Among which, Zang Kejia's *Selected New Poems of China (1919-1949)* and *Fifty saffron flowers (poems of fifty foreign poets)* translated by Yuan ShuiPai,[2] aroused his love of poetry and had a great influence on him. At the same time, he also composed a lot of poems and songs, and even compiled four collections of poems for himself, including The

1 Tian Zhonghe: "Happy because of Literature - Preface to 'The Sun of Tomorrow'", in The Sun of Tomorrow, Henan People's Publishing House, 2014, p. 1.

2 In the first data sent by Tanaka Wo to the author, the translator was mistakenly written as Guo Moruo, but after the author verified, it should be Yuan Shui Pao, so he corrected it. However, when the author sent the revised draft to Tian Zhonghe for review, he changed the name of Yuan Shubai to Guo Moruo again, saying that he remembered it that way. After the author verified Yuan Shui Pao again and talked with Tian Zhonghe on the phone, he finally confirmed that it was a mistake in his memory. The author has repeated this detail here, not to show how rigorous he is, but to say that memory is sometimes so tenacious, but also to remind scholars of the memoirs of writers to maintain due vigilance on the content of memoirs.

Morning Bell Collection, *The Morning Bell Sequel*, *The Morning Bell Three Collections*, and *The Crying of Blood*, all of which were unpublished.

1957, at the age of seventeen

He was transferred to the newly built First Industrial and Agricultural Middle School of Henan Province (now Zhengzhou Seventh Middle School). During this period, Tian Zhonghe read the Indian epic *Shakuntala*. This book had a great influence on Tian Zhonghe's literary concept and literary creation. "Shakuntala made me understand what poetry is and what the charm of literature is, so I said goodbye to Mayakovsky and Guo Xiaochuan, whom I used to love and admire very much, and immersed myself in Indian literature for the whole summer vacation."[1] "Gari Tosha and Rabindranath Tagore built a Noah's Ark for me with their poems and songs, so that I would not be depressed or discouraged during the next twenty years of my life, and I would keep my enthusiasm alive. This is the power of truth, goodness and beauty, the power of human passion and dignity."[2] In the summer of the same year, Tian Zhonghe systematically read Shakespeare's works. His sonnets are unforgettable. After reading *Romeo and Juliet*, *Hamlet*, *Othello*, and *The Merchant of Venice* in a single breath, poetry and history, story and life were dissolved into a sweet wine in the power of language.[3]

1958, at the age of eighteen

In the summer vacation of that year, Tian Zhonghe went back to his hometown in Tanghe to visit his cousin's aunt who was sick. "When I went back to school, I saw my aunt's thin, withered and wrinkled face, and the slop-like medicine in the tiled basin. Soon after, my aunt passed away.

---

1 Tian Zhonghe, "From Shakuntalo to Twenty-two Rules of War," World Literature, No. 6, 2001.

2 Same as ②.

3 Tian Zhonghe: "From Shakuntalo to Twenty-two Military Rules", World Literature, No. 6, 2001

However, the story told by my aunt lingered in my heart for a long time, and during the winter vacation, I conceived and wrote a long poem, *The Immortal Flower*." [1]

1959, at the age of 19

In May, the long poem *Immortal Flower* was published by Henan People's Publishing House. "This children's poem is about a young man Xu Quan, who, after his parents died of a spreading plague in his village, decided to look for the magic elixir to cure his fellow townspeople's illnesses. With kindness and bravery, he overcame the storm and the cold, and the greedy and vicious villagers, fetched the elixir flowers, and restored the health of the whole village." [2] Regarding the publishing process, the author once recalled: "It was the third year of high school. One Sunday, I took my fairy tale poem and went to visit the holy place in my heart——The Henan Provincial Federation of Literature located in the Workers' New Village. There, I met Ms. Ding Lin who was on duty. She gave me a lecture on Bian Zhilin's poems and kept my long poem. A week later, I received a letter from the Henan People's Publishing House, saying that they had decided to publish the book." [3]

In that year, Tian Zhonghe graduated from Zhengzhou No. 7 Middle School and enrolled in the Lanzhou Arts Academy[4], which had just been

1 Tian Zhonghe: "Flowers and Youth and Spring", in Tongshizhai Notes: Flower and Youth, Elephant Press, 2019, p. 344.

2 Tian Zhonghe, "Flowers and Youth and Spring", in Tongshizhai Notes: Flower and Youth, Elephant Press, 2019, p. 344.

3 Tian Zhonghe: "Literature and Happiness - Prologue to 'The Sun of Tomorrow'", in The Sun of Tomorrow, Henan People's Publishing House, 2014, p. 1.

4 In 1958, Lanzhou Academy of Arts was formed by the merger of the Chinese Department of Lanzhou University, the Art Department of Northwest Normal College, and the Cadre School of Culture and Arts of Gansu Province. In 1962, the Lanzhou College of Arts was abolished, the Chinese Department of Lanzhou University was reintegrated into Lanzhou University, and the Fine Arts and Music Departments were merged into the Gansu Normal University (now the Northwest Normal University). Tian Zhonghe's withdrawal certificate was issued by Lanzhou University, so in Tian Zhonghe's official

established in 1958. In Tian Zhonghe's mind, Lanzhou Arts College did not seem to be ideal, "The high-minded and proud me failed to enter the ideal university because of my second brother's complicity, and the brilliant sky above my head became cloudy and confused in an instant".[1] Tian Zhonghe also gave little account of his life during his university years.

1960, at the age of twenty

In May, *Fairyland Flowers* was reprinted.

1961, at the age of twenty-one

After the reprinting, *Fairyland Flowers* was selected by the Ministry of Culture to be exhibited in the Paris International Children's Book Fair, and later it was included in *Selected Children's Literature of Henan in the Decade (1949-1959)* published by Henan People 's Publishing House.

1962, at the age of twenty-two

In March, he dropped out of the Chinese Department of Lanzhou University. Fifty years later, Tian Zhonghe fondly recalled the scene when he left Lanzhou: "I suddenly thought of that cold spring night, when a group of university students, carrying bags and net bags, surrounded by a handsome young man, walked into the freight gate of Lanzhou East Station. They followed the railroad tracks that glittered in the darkness, found the eastbound train, and clamored and wished in front of the compartment. The boy set down his baggage and waved goodbye to his classmates from the window of the train, full of joy and excitement, like a chivalrous man with a sword, a bird flying out of a cage."[2] It is said that he also had a good time with his

---

introduction and curriculum vitae, his academic qualifications are listed as "incomplete studies at the Chinese Department of Lanzhou University".

1 Tian Zhonghe, "From 'Shakung Daro' to 'Twenty-two Military Rules'", World Literature, No. 6, 2001.

2 Tian Zhonghe: "How am I Living in the Twenty-first Century?

classmates. It is said that he also "wrote a little poem to his classmates in the dim light of the car as a farewell, which reads: The night is closing in / I will see the sun of my hometown when I wake up.[1]

In May, he went to Tangzhuang village of Gezhai brigade in the suburbs of Zhengzhou city to work as a farmer. After settling down, Tian Zhonghe participated in the labor of the production team and kept reading and writing at the same time. In just two years, he finished his senior year of university, wrote two long poems, "Springtime on the Jialu River" and "Song of the Golden Pipa", three collections of short poems, and the first four chapters of a full-length novel, *The Running of the Jialu River*. However, for various reasons, none of these works were published at that time.

In that year, Tian Zhonghe married Han Jinrong. Han Jinrong was one year younger than Tian Zhonghe, and her temperament was as romantic as Tian Zhonghe's. She wrote several short poems during the wedding, among which is

"Send Two Peach Blossoms". She writes: "After leaving the branch, my life is thin, and I have withered among the barren grasses since then". "Mother and wife are the two great women in Tian Zhonghe's life and career." 2

1964, at the age of twenty-four

In August, he left Zhengzhou and settled down in Xinyang. For denouncing the branch secretary who was the chief of the supply and marketing section of the purchase of industrial alcohol collaborating with a factory in Zhengzhou City to illegally purchase industrial alcohol to pass off as baijiu, Tian Zhonghe was retaliated against, and he could not continue to live in Ge

1 Nanding, "The Romantic Tian Zhonghe", Chinese Writers, No.1, 1995.
2 Nanding, "The Romantic Tian Zhonghe", Chinese Writers, No. 1, 1995.

Zhai, he had no choice but went to Liulipeng village (now Shihe District Liulipeng community) to run to his sister and her husband. He lived in the production team's cattle house. While living in Xinyang, Tianzhonghe and his wife became part-time teachers and actively learn Chairman Mao's writing and thought. During the break between work and labor, Tian Zhonghe continued to be creative in literature and read famous books.

1968, at the age of twenty-eight

In December, they left Xinyang and went back to their hometown in Tanghe. Tian Zhonghe and his wife, who could not live in Xinyang, returned to Tanghe County. Because it coincided with the urban population going to the countryside, they temporarily lived in Dazhang town, Tian Zhonghe's rural hometown, in the kitchen of one of his nephews.

1972, at the age of thirty-two

In October, due to the "implementation of the policy of citizens going to the countryside", Tian Zhonghe and his family went back to the city in Tanghe County, where the couple became teachers. When the couple failed to pass the political examination, they failed to become permanent staff and were dismissed from their job as part-time teachers. Since then, Tian Zhonghe had been wandering in Henan and Hubei. "It was a time when he was in desperation and on tenterhooks, and he was barely securing a career to support his family, sometimes wandering, and sometimes doing odd jobs in factories. He not only had to submit one yuan and twenty cents a day, but also had to pay management fees. Late at night, often the street cadres suddenly knocked on the door with a flashlight, broke into our bedroom to check the account, questioned friends and relatives who occasionally stayed there, and searched through their clothes..."[1].

---

1 Tian Zhonghe, "A Tree in the Old Garden", in A Tree in the Old Garden, Haiyan Publishing House, 2001, p. 20.

1980, at the age of forty

He was rehabilitated.

1981, at the age of forty-one

In January, he joined the Tanghe County Cultural Center. Tian Zhonghe called the period from 1962, when he dropped out of Lanzhou University on his own initiative, to 1981, when he worked at the Tanghe County Cultural Center as the twenty years of "self-exile". "Without these twenty years of wandering life, my works would never have such a deep and painful sense of vicissitudes. As I said earlier, I am not pessimistic, nor have I ever despaired, I have only been able to face up to the inequalities and sufferings of the human world after enriching my experience, and I have a stronger sense of criticism.[1] ② While working at the Museum of Culture, Tian Zhonghe read *Catch-22*. This book gave him a great shock and even changed his view of literature to a certain extent. "When I finished twenty years of wandering ...... and was struggling to find books to read, I found a copy of *Catch-22* in the small library of our cultural center.

This book really blew me away ...... The reality of Shakuntalo is the reality of young boys and girls, while the reality of *Catch-22* is the reality of the adult world. Shakuntalo moved me, and *Catch-22* inspired me. Like the thirst I had at the age of sixteen, *Catch-22* aroused in me a second hunger for reading. ...... Starting from Baudelaire and Eliot, I read one topic, one topic, one author, one author, just as I did when I first came down from the university.[2]

In March, the poem "Poems from Lu Xun's Residence" (three poems) was published in the 3rd issue of Luoshen.

---

1 Miao Meiling and Tian Zhonghe, "Walking Freely in the Scene of Literature - An Interview with Tian Zhonghe", Dongjing Literature, No. 3, 2012.
2 Tian Zhonghe, "From Shakung Daro to Catch-22", World Literature, No. 6, 2001.

In September, the poem "Lu Xun's Eyes" was published in People's Daily on September 10th.

1982, at the age of forty-two

He published the short story "A Newsman in a Small Town" (*Garden of Flowers*, No.4), the short story "Jade Pigeon" (*Garden of Flowers*, No.5), the short story "Dreams Dissipate in the Morning Sunshine" (*Gong Geng Magazine*, No.7-8), and the short story "Sycamore Courtyard" (*Gong Geng Magazine*, No.10).

1983, at the age of forty-three

He published the short story "Two Rows of Wheat" (*Garden of Flowers*, No. 3), "The Distant Shore of the Other Side of the River" (*Garden of Flowers*, No. 7), and "The Moon Goes Away, and I Go Away Too" (*Contemporary*, No. 4).

In the same year, Zeng Fan published the literary review "Impressions of Tian Zhonghe's Novels" (*Garden of Flowers*, No.11), which is probably the earliest literary review on Tian Zhonghe's work.

1984, at the age of forty-four

In the spring of that year, Tian Qin, the mother of Tian Zhonghe, died at the age of eighty-two.[1] When my mother passed away, "the mourners crowded my yard and the path in front of my house, and almost all the old friends and neighbors in the street bid her farewell with sincere respect. At that moment, I was proud of my mother's ordinary life". Summing up the

---

1 In "Tian Zhonghe's Family Profile," Tian Qin's birth and death dates are clearly stated as: "Born on the fifteenth day of the eleventh month of the lunar calendar in 1903 (the year of the rabbit, the decanate year), and died on the ninth day of the third month of the year 1984 (the seventh day of the second month of the year of the jiazi year)." According to the weekly age calculation method, Tian Qin should have been 81 years old when he died, but in all of the author's narratives, this age is 82 years old, which is obviously contradictory to his calculation of the ages of his father, his eldest sister, his sixth sister, and so on.

reason why her mother won such respect and fame in the countryside, Tian Zhonghe said, "Perhaps it was the many hardships of life and her strong, confident and self-reliant character that made her who she was."[1] The departure of his mother plunged Tian Zhonghe into deep sorrow. "Although she left me at the age of eighty-two, I still could not accept the reality of losing my mother. I did not have the heart to study and I could not write until half a year later when I slowly came out of the grief.[2] Mother was not only Tian Zhonghe's first teacher, but also the person who influenced him the most. "My mother's self-respect and love of life have been the spiritual pillar of my difficult years." "My mother, who is kind, wise, strong, upright, passionate, cheerful, helpful, and rich, has left a rich nourishment for me.[3] Such a mother figure has appeared repeatedly in many of Tian Zhonghe's literary works, and has become a persistent theme in his literary creation, which mainly include:the short story collections, *Fallen Leaf Creek*, and long novels, *The Bandit Chief*, *Seventeen*, and *Father and Them*.

1985, at the age of forty-five

The short story "May" was published in the 5th issue of *Shanxi Literature*. "May" is written from a human point of view, starting from the anguish and family conflicts in the harvest season, in order to leave a true picture of history. For the sake of authenticity, it chooses the most common farmhouse and the most ordinary life, does not create sensational plots, does not carry out pioneering explorations in form, and lets the whole text present a calm and peaceful outlook."[4] Some critics think that May represents the highest

---

1 Tian Zhonghe, "Spring Thoughts," in A Tree in the Old Garden, Haiyan Publishing House, 2001, p. 29.
2 Tian Zhonghe, "Eternal Consolation," in Tong Shi Zhai Notes: Flowers and Youth, Elephant Press, 2019, p. 101.
3 Tian Zhonghe: "Spring Thoughts", in A Tree in the Old Garden, Haiyan Publishing House, 2001, p. 31.
4 Tian Zhonghe: "Forever Consolation", in Tongshizhai Notes: Flower and Youth, Elephant Publishing House, 2019, p. 102.

achievement of Tian Zhonghe's realism. "The novel demonstrates Tian Zhonghe's keen sense of realism and deep insight. The novel tears away the rich and glamorous canvas of rural real life, removes the bright halo that has long been over the heads of modern villages and peasants, and reveals the original face of contemporary rural real life. More importantly, and what makes the work the most realistic is that it avoids the optimistic and romantic mood of the rural novels under the influence of the world trend, and reveals with sincerity the mistakes of the Party's policies and the loss and damage caused to the production and life of contemporary farmers."[1]

Other important works published in this year include the short stories "Sophora Shadow" (*Shanghai Literature*, No.1), "Flowerless Spring" (*Mangyuan*, No. 6), and the short story "This Side of the Mountain" (*Benliu*, No. 10). In that year, research papers on Tian Zhonghe included Zhang Shishan's "Ripening in the Harvest Season - Reading Tian Zhonghe's May", *Red Flag*, No. 15.

1986, at the age of forty-six

In February, he was transferred to the Tanghe County Literature Federation and became its vice-chairman.

The short story "May" won the Shanxi Literature Prize, the short story "Spring Day" won the Running Stream Prize for Outstanding Work, and the medium-length story "Flowerless Spring" won the Mangyuan Prize for Outstanding Work.

The main works published in this year are: short story "Spring Day" (*Benliu*, No.3), creative talk "I Write May" (*Literary Knowledge*, No.6), short story "Chun Gugu" (*Benliu*, No.7), novella "Autumn" (*Shanxi Literature*,

---

1 Zhang Shuheng, "The Pioneering Nature of Non-Pioneers - On Tian Zhonghe's Creative Transformation in the Nineties", Journal of Henan Normal University (Philosophy and Social Science Edition), No. 5, 1999.

No.10), and commentary "Literature's Rural, Philosophical, and Worldly Character" (*Benliu*, No.12).

1987, at the age of forty-seven

In July, through the efforts of Nanding, the then chairman of the Henan Provincial Literature Federation, and Su Jinshou, a veteran poet, Tian Zhonghe was transferred to the Henan Provincial Literature Federation and became a professional writer.

The series of short stories *Fallen Leaf Creek* (five works, including "Glass Milk", "Human Head Li", "Zhou Xianggong", "Eighth Aunt" and "Rice Soup Aunt") was published in *Shanghai Literature*, No. 12. Starting from the series of short stories, an important area of Tian Zhonghe's literary creation gradually appeared, that is, his hometown and relatives. In the following thirty years of his writing career, the subject matter and style of Tian Zhonghe's creative work have changed a lot, from the traditional realism facing the present, to the "new realism", "new history" and other chapters with a modernized color, Tian Zhonghe has been pursuing the breakthrough and innovation possibilities of his own self. However, there is one field that has never been interrupted, and the prose culture style of his writing also runs through, that is, the creation of his hometown and relatives, which finally became a big scene, became an important achievement of Tian Zhonghe's creation in his later years, and he published the full-length novels *Seventeen*, and *Father and Them*.

The main research papers on Tian Zhobghe in that year include: Zheng Boguang, "From 'May' to 'Autumn': A Review of Two Novels by Tian Zhonghe(Commentary)," *Shanxi Literature*, Issue 4; Zhao Fusheng, "Wandering Between Fear and Hope: Random Thoughts on Tanaka He's Novels," *Benliu*, Issue 6; Cao Zengyu, "Focusing on and Examining the Souls of the Weak: A Brief Discussion of Tian Zhonghe's Novels," *Benliu*, Issue 6.

1988, at the age of forty-eight

The short story "May" won the 8th (1985-1986) National Outstanding Short Novel Award. Among the 19 novels that won the award, "May" topped the list with unanimous votes. At the same time, the works of Henan writers selected for this award include "Full Ticket" by Qiao Shenyun and "Han's Daughter" by Zhou Daxin.

The short story "The Last Autumn Rain" was published in the 12th issue of *People's Literature.*

Tian Zhonghe's works in this period not only changed his writing techniques, but also probed into the depths of the hearts of the rural youths. "Artistically speaking, Tian Zhonghe's creation presents a huge metaphorical space behind the surface structure of the story, which allows us to deeply experience the mutation of human nature, the blindness of the society, the chaos of life in this era, in a word: the phenomenon of the changes of history." [1] They are "puzzles and worries about the cultural disorder".[2]

Other major works published in the same year included the short story series *Fallen Leaf Creek* (two works, including 'Poppy' and "Mr. Huo," published in *Beijing Literature*, Issue 7).

1989, at the age of forty-nine

The novel *Tomorrow's Sun* was published in *Shanghai Literature*, No.6. The focus of the novel is shifted to the fate of urban youth, and the writing method is gradually shifted from traditional realism to "new realism", which can be regarded as the second change of Tian Zhonghe's creation. The novel was well-received and won the fourth Shanghai Literature Prize after its

---

1 Wu Bingjie, "Discovering a New Continent: A Discussion of Tian Zhonghe's Recent Works", *Contemporary Writers' Review*, No. 4, 1989.
2 Chen Jihui: "Confusion and Worry about Cultural Disorder - The Significance of Tian Zhonghe's Recent Works", *Literary Review*, No. 1, 1990.

release. Some of Tian Zhonghe's novels of this period were also categorized by critics as "new realistic novels".

Other major works published in this year include the novella "The Peach Tree" (*October*, No.1); the novella "South Wind" (*Contemporary*, No.1), and the short story series

Fallen Leaf Creek (three works, including "Ghost Festival", "Quail", "Bookshop Ran", *Contemporary Writers*, No. 2); the novella "Liu Huo" (*Mangyuan*, No. 2), the creative talk "Listening to the groans of humanity under the wheels of the historical car" (*Mangyuan*, No. 2), the creative talk "You do not have to care too much, nor do you have to ......" (*Selected Novels*, No. 3), creative talk "Believe in the future" (*Selected Novels*, No. 6), prose "At the cut-off point between history and humanity to look at the countryside" (*Selected Novels*, No. 6), and essay "Viewing the Countryside at the Cutting Point of History and Humanity" (*Shanxi Literature*, Issue 12).

The main research papers on Tian Zhonghe in that year include: Hu Wen, "The Smashed Psychological Reality - Reading The Last Autumn Rain", No. 2, *Fiction Review*; Song Suiliang, "Sinking-Confusion-Grief - Review of Three Recent Writings of Tian Zhonghe", No. 3, *Review of Contemporary Writers*; Wu Bingjie, "Discovering a New Continent Tian Zhonghe's Recent Works", No. 4, *Review of Contemporary Writers*; Zhou Yi, "Writers Should Have a Self-conscious Sense of Social Responsibility - Tian Zhonghe's Evening Talks", *Literary Gazette*, No. 9; and Siqing, "The True Colors of Life: A Reading of Tian Zhonghe's 'Tomorrow's Sun'", *Fiction Review*, No. 5.

1990, at the age of fifty years old

The Chinese novel *Tomorrow's Sun* was awarded the Fourth Shanghai Literature Prize.

The main works published in this year are: the Chinese novel *Graveyard* (*Contemporary*, No. 1), the short story *Grassland - Riverland* (*Mangyuan*, No. 1), the novel *Bombardment* (*Harvest*, No. 5), the short story series Fallen Leaf Creek (two works, including “Gua Da”, “painter Li”) (*Contemporary Novels*, No. 9), the short story series *Fallen Leaf Creek* (four works, including “the Memory of Tsubaki”, “Auntie Cousin”, “The Green Door”, “Lan Yun”, *Shanghai Literature*, No.11), and the short story, *The Grassland* (*People’s Literature*, No.12).

Research papers on Tian Zhonghe in that year include: Chen Jihui, “Confusion and Worry about Cultural Disorder - The Significance of Tian Zhonghe’s Recent Works”, *Literary Review*, No.1; Zhang Dexiang, “The Atmosphere of the Times and the Sorrows and Happiness of the Farmhouse - A Review of Tian Zhonghe’s middle-grade novel ‘The Peach Tree’”, *Contemporary Literature*, No.2; Zhang Dexiang, “The Realistic Changes and the Ideal Personality - Review of Tian Zhonghe’s Two Chinese Novels”, *Fiction Review*, No.2; Duan Chongxuan, “Tian Zhonghe and His ‘Human World’”, *Shanghai Literature*, No.8.

1991, 51 years old

The main works published in this year include the short story “Yuanheng Hao and Shi Yi De Merchants” (*Contemporary Writers*, No.1), the short story series *Fallen Leaf Creek* (three works, including “The Fuchsia Beauty”, “Lu Qisan”, and “Oleander ”, *People’s Literature*, No.6), and the review “The Short Novels and the Menjie Sponges” (*Shanxi Literature*, No.8).

The research papers on Tian Zhonghe in the same year include Duan Chongxuan’s “Alloy Gold Style Literature - Talking about the Artistic Expression of Tian Zhonghe’s Novels”, *Fiction Review*, No. 2.

1992, 52 years old

The short story "May" won the first Henan Provincial Outstanding Literary and Artistic Achievement Award, and the short story series *Fallen Leaf Creek* (three works) won the annual Tianjin Literature Award.

The first draft of the novel *Walled city*①[1]was published in the 3rd issue, *Huacheng* in 1992. *The Bandit Chief* was written between 1990 and 1992, coinciding with the revival of long novel writing; the first draft of *Walled City* was published in *Huacheng*, Issue No. 3, 1992,

Three months before the novel was published by Shanghai Literature and Art Publishing House, Tian Zhonghe made two-thirds of the changes to the novel, retaining the backbone of the story, and strengthening the poetic qualities of the language."[2] "The moralistic life story, the distinctive folklore, the prose language, the impressionistic mood, the symbolism, and the new structural form, make this long novel of high artistic quality."[3] *The Bandit Chief* and *Bombardment* and *Heavenly Realm* and other works had been categorized by critics as "New Historical Novels", and their appearances also heralded another transformation of Tian Zhonghe's creation.

The main works published in this year also include: "*Heavenly Realm*"(*Novelist*, No.1), "*Fallen Leaf Creek*" (third work with the same title, including "Impression of the Ancestral Hall", "Horse Dung Li Village" and "Tangled River") (*Hot Wind*, No.1), the novella "The Restoration of the First Element" (*Mangyuan*, No. 2), "Fallen Leaves Stream" (third work with the same title, including "Two Degrees of Plum", "Lv Liansheng" and "The First

---

1 The novel was renamed Bandit Chief when it was published by Shanghai Literature and Art Publishing House in 1994.

2 He Xiangyang: "A Cultural Retelling of Sensual History - The Bandit Chief: A Taste of Exile", *Novel Review*, No.1, 1995.

3 Liu Xuelin, "Tian Zhonghe - The Story of Expedition or on the Road", *Beijing Literature*, No. 8, 2001.

Step-Sister") (*Tianjin Literature*, No.2), and the novella "Impressions" (*Novelist* No. 6).

1993, 53 years old

In July, a collection of short story and novellas, *Moonlight Goes, I Go Too*, was published by Writers Publishing House, which was the first collection of Tian Zhonghe's works.

Other major works published in this year include the short story series "Fallen Leaf Creek" (two works, including "Hanging" and "Throwing into the River", *Shanxi Literature*, No. 2), and the short story seris " Fallen Leaf Creek" (two works, including "Stone Seal Pavilion" and "The Three Masterpiece of Archway Street", *Chinese Writers*, No. 2),

Dialogues: Human Nature and Realism (Dialogue with Mo Bai, *Literary Free Talk*, No.2), novella *The Same Moonlight* (*Yellow River*, No.2), Review *Lost in Your Own Heart* (*Novelist*, No.4), Short Stories Fallen Leaf Creek (two works, including *The Memory of Malaria*, *Horseman and Scabies and Tea Shop*, *Zhongshan Literary Bimonthly*, No.3), Short Stories *Fallen Leaf Creek* (two works, including *Pomegranate Sisters*, *Brothers Ma*, *Tianjin Literature*, No.7), Dialogues Definition of Works and Three Domains of Literature - Creative Correspondence, *Tianjin Literature*, No.3), Dialogues Positioning of Works and the Three Fields of Literature - Creative Correspondence (*Novelist*, No. 5), and the essays "Chatting in the Gentlemen' Parlor" (*World Literature*, No. 6).

1994, 54 years old

The essay "Chatting in a Gentleman's Parlor" won the Essay Prize of World Literature.

In February, *The Bandit Chief* was published by Shanghai Literary and Art Publishing House, as part of the "Literature Library of the Novel World" series of long novels. The famous novels included in this library include Zhang Wei's *September Fable* and *The Family*, Li Rui's The Old Site, Zhang Jie's "No Characters", Han Shaogong's "The Ma Qiao Dictionary", Shi Tiesheng's Notes on the Abstract, Lu Tianming's "The Sky is Above", and You Fengwei's "China 1957", etc.

The main works published in this year are: the short story *Fallen Leaf Creek* (two works, including "Puji Pharmacy" and "Clock Shop", *Tianjin Literature*, No. 4), the essay "Elegant and Dashing Escape" (*Essay*, No. 3), and the short story "Wandering Breeder" (*Mangyuan*, No. 4).

1995, 55 years old

The long novel *The Bandit Chief* won the second Henan Provincial Outstanding Literary and Artistic Achievement Award. The main works published in this year include: creation talk "The Adventure of Super Mari - Notes on the Creation of 'The Bandit Chief'" (*Fiction Review*, No.1), short story "The Mill Workshop of Xu Family" (*Literary World*, No.1), review "White Pagoda Made of Lettuce" (*People's Literature*, No.10), prose "Pendulum-Leaves-Human Nature's Magnetic Poles" (*Essay*, No.6), and dialogue "More Consciously Pursue Aesthetic Values - Dialogue on Long Story 'The Bandit Chief'" (Sun Sun and Tian Zhonghe, *Henan Daily*, December 22, 1995).

The research papers on Tian Zhonghe in that year mainly include: Du Tiancai, "The Bandit Chief: A New Artistic World", *Fiction Review*, No.1; He Xiangyang, "Cultural Restatement of Sensual History - The Bandit Chief: A Taste of Exile", *Fiction Review*, No.1; He Qiusheng, "Summary of the Seminar on Tian Zhonghe's Long Story 'The Bandit Chief'", *Fiction Review*, No.1; and Nanding, "The Romantic Tian Zhonghe", *Chinese Writers*, No.1.

1996, 56 years old

Tian Zhonghe became vice chairman of Henan Provincial Federation of Literature, chairman of Henan Provincial Writers' Association, member of the National Committee of Chinese Writers' Association.

In January, a collection of short and medium-length novels called "Impression" was published by Shanghai Literature and Art Publishing House, which is one of the series of short and medium-sized novels in the "Fiction World Library". Other famous short stories included in this library include Feng Jijiwei's *The Tall Woman and Her Short Husband*, Deng Youmei's *The Smoking Pot*, Zhang Xianliang's *Shorbulaq*, Liu Shaotang's *Four or Five Families in a Foggy Village*, and Wang Anyi's *Town of Little Bao*.

The main works published in this year include the short story "The Experience of Homicide" (*People's Literature*, No. 3), and the creative talk "Breakthrough in Silence" (*People's Daily*, April 4, 1996)、 essay "Sin, Suffering and Strength" (*Chinese Reading News*, April 17), short story "Unknown Night Visitor" (*Tianjin Literature*, No. 4), review "The Spirit and Countermeasures to Reality" (*Literature and Arts Newspaper*, May 17), short story "Nomad's Little Story" (*Mangyuan*, No. 3), essay "Reading Music (Two Issues)" (*Essay*, No. 4), short story "Sister's Village" (*Shanxi Literature*, No.11), creative talk "Countryside: Cultural Specimen of the Original Ecology" (*Shanxi Literature*, No. 11).

1997, 57 years old

In May, the collection *Fallen Leaf Creek* was published by Henan Literary and Art Publishing House, which contains 38 reminiscence essay-style novels by Tian Zhonghe with the local customs of his hometown as the background. The reminiscent mood, the style of prose, the leisurely tone, and the people in the small town with rich local flavor, make the readers naturally immerse themselves in the historical flavor and real life of the small town in

South Henan Province. According to Zheng Shusen, *Fallen Leaf Creek* "emphasizes mood and painstakingly cares about wording", and "is a successful model for transforming the tradition of local novels.[1] Tian Zhonghe seemed to take this evaluation seriously, citing it more than once, arguing that the series of novels *Fallen Leaf Creek* was valued "probably because the series tells poetic stories about human nature in the countryside, and it transcends politics and comes closer to the essence of literature"[2]. Zheng Shusen's comment brought two inspirations to Tian Zhonghe: firstly, it strengthened his long-held notion that human nature is the essence of literature, and facilitated a complete change of his focus from society to human nature. Another inspiration was the negative awakening, which prompted Tian Zhonghe to reflect on the tradition and to explore modern techniques and texts. Tian Zhonghe believed that he should not only be able to transform local novels, but also be able to create his own modernist works. After the 1990s, he became more conscious of deviating from mainstream writing, counteringsocial writing with humanistic writing, and traditional narrative with textual innovation, and his writing's literary form underwent greatly changes. These two points became the watershed of Tian Zhonghe's successful escape from mainstream writing. In this sense, the negative awakening of Zheng Shusen's evaluation seems to be more important. [3]

In August, *Bombardment*, a collection of short and medium-sized stories, was published by Huaxia Publishing House. This collection of short stories is part of the "Chinese Contemporary Writers' Library" edited by Mr. Zhang Qie, a famous literary critic. Other famous writers whose works are included in this library include Li Peifu's *The Sheep's Door*, *The Boundless Morning*,

1 Zheng Shusen, The Weeping Window - Selected Novels of Mainland China in the Eighties - Preface, Hongfan Bookstore, 1990, p. 5.
2 Miao Meiling and Tian Zhonghe, "Walking Freely in the Scene of Literature - An Interview with Tian Zhonghe", Dongjing Literature, No. 3, 2012.
3 These two inspirations were expressed by Mr. Tian Zhonghe in the process of communication with the author.

Jia Ping'wa's *White Night, Shangzhou: Untold Stories (four volumes),* Lu Yao's *The Ordinary World,* Zhang Wei's *Can't Remember Sichuan Sunflower*, and Chen Zhongshi's *White Deer Plains*, etc.

Research papers on Tian Zhonghe in that year mainly include Wang Min's "A Deep Analysis of China's Rural Areas in the Era of Change - An Experimental Discussion of Tian Zhonghe's Novel Writing", *Journal of Henan Normal University* (Philosophy and Social Science Edition), No. 3.

1998, 58 years old

In September, *Tian Zhonghe's Selected Novels* was published by Henan Literary Arts Publishing House. It is part of the "Nanyang Writers' Group Series". The series mainly includes: Qiao DianYun's Selected Novels, Zhang Yigong's Selected Novels, Zhou Daxin's Selected Novels, February River's Selected Novels, Tian Zhonghe's Selected Novels, Zhou Tongbin's Selected Prose, etc.

1999, 59 years old

The main works published in this year are: the novel *Go to Jail* (*Chinese Writers*, No. 1), the novella *White Heart Traces* (*Mangyuan*, No. 2), the novella *Grandfather's Coffin and Grandmother's Donkey* (*People's Literature*, No. 4), the short story *The Story of Coming into the World* (*Shanghai Literature*, No. 8), and the novel *Dates and Grains of the Year 1944* (*Zhongshan Literary Bimonthly*, No. 6).

The main research papers on Tian Zhonghe in that year are: Mei Huilan, "Mother: The Everlasting Undertone of Life - An Essay on Tian Zhonghe's Creative Work", *Fiction Review*, No.4; Zhang Shuheng, "A Brief Discussion on Tian Zhonghe's Novel Creation", *Academic Forum of Nandu*, No.4; Zhang Shuheng, "The Pioneering of Non-Pioneering - On the Creative Transformation of Tian Zhonghe in the Nineties", *Henan Normal University Journal* (Philosophy and Social Science Edition), No.5.

2000, 60 years old

The main works published in this year are: short story "Kinsman" (two works, *Novelist*, No. 3), essay "Prepare your inn" (*Essay Selection*, No. 4), novella "The marriage of Sister Sixth" (*Oasis*, No. 5), novella "Suddenly far away" (*Mangyuan*, No.5), essay "Fine Arts and Literature" (six articles, *Mangyuan*, No. 1- 6).

2001, 61 years old

In March, the collection *A Tree in the Old Garden* was published by Haiyan Publishing House. The genre of this collection is not easy to determine, and it was named by the editors as "reminiscent language", which is a form of writing in the late Chinese literature, "sometimes called notebooks, sometimes treated as novels, and its main feature is to recall the past, and to feel the love of relatives".[1] The collection consists of three parts, each of which contains six chapters, among which the chapters in "My Family Stories" are either left intact, or re-titled, or reorganized and incorporated into the full-length novel *Seventeen*. From this, we can see that the novel *Seventeen* has a strong autobiographical color, and can even be regarded as the author's documentary memoir to a certain extent.

Other major works published in this year include an essay published in the 6th issue of *World Literature*, "From 'Shakuntalo' to 'Catch-22'", which is of great significance to the understanding of Tian Zhonghe's reading perspective and the formation of his literary concepts.

The main research papers on Tian Zhonghe in this year include: Chen Jihui and Cao Jianling, "History, Humanity and Poetic Vision: Tian Zhonghe's Literary World", *Zhengzhou University Journal* (Philosophy and

1 The short story collection Fallen Leaf Creek was awarded the Third Henan Provincial Excellent Artistic Achievement, and the essay Concealment and Deception in the State of Manners was awarded the First Prize in the Prose Competition of the Chinese Prose Society.

Social Science Edition), No.1; Liu Xuelin, "Tian Zhonghe - A Story of Adventure or on the Road", *Beijing Literature* (Wonderful Readings), No.8.

2003, 63 years old

The collection of short stories *Fallen Leaf Creek* won the Third Henan Provincial Excellent Literary and Artistic Achievements, essay "On Deception and Fraud in a Nation of Etiquette" won the first prize in the Chinese Essay Association's Essay Competition.

Novella "Lucky, Good Luck!" was published in the 2nd issue of *Great Wall*. "Lucky, Good Luck!" and seven other short stories, including "The Killing Experience", "The Unknown Night Visitor", "Nomad's Novel", "Sister's Village", "Go to Jail", and "Neon Lights at Dusk", which are called the "Urban Myths Series", are a group of "experimental novels". According to the writer himself, the purpose of writing this group of novels is to prove his "creativity", "seven works with seven techniques, completely breaking the style of Fallen Leaf Creek". Although the author admits that "this decade of exploration has indeed made me stray from the attention of critics", he insists that "it is precisely this period of unnoticed works that marks my artistic maturity. I believe that history will prove this in the future. This group of works is all about the survival of the grassroots people in the economic tide, the depression and the distortion of the spirit of the current situation. It inherits the sense of sorrow of *May*, deepens the theme of the destruction of human nature by society, and makes a more complete betrayal of the mainstream literature and the main theme. This is a kind of non-utilitarian writing. Artistically it is purer and ideologically it is more critical"[1].

1 Miao Meiling and Tian Zhonghe, "Walking Freely in the Scene of Literature: An Interview with Tian Zhonghe", Dongjing Literature, No. 3, 2012.

2004, 64 years old

Research papers on Tian Zhonghe in that year include: Li Shaoyong, "Constructing a Poetics of Dream - On Tian Zhonghe's Novel Creation", Journal of Zhoukou Normal College, No.1; Wu Xiaoyan, "Aesthetic Presentation of Folk Myths – Brief Comment on Tian Zhonghe's The Bandit Chief", *Fiction Review*, No. 4; Liu Yongchun, "Local Feeling and Life Condition - On Tian Zhonghe's Folk Writing", *Fiction Review*, No. 5.

2007, 67 years old

The major works published in this year include the novella "The Progressive Tian Qin" (*Works*, No.4), and the creation talk "The Individual, the Supreme Protagonist of Literature" (*Works*, No.4).

The main research papers on Tian Zhonghe in that year were Liu Haiyan's "When Fantasy Seeps into the Writer's Blood", *Works*, No. 4.

2010, 70 years old

In March, the long novel *Seventeen* was published in the 2nd issue of Chinese Writers. The novel consists of a diary and fourteen short and medium articles, which are independent of each other and have human connections, and many of them have been published as novels or even memoir essays. Therefore, although it can be regarded as a novel, it can also be regarded as the autobiography of Tian Zhonghe's adolescence to a certain extent. In an interview, Tian Zhonghe said frankly: "*Seventeen* can be regarded as my autobiography. You can see my childhood in it, thus you can see the experience of my inner growth and the spiritual factors of the formation of my writing style."[1] The novel traces the long story of the youthful years of the six members of the family, including 'me', in a secure and graspable tone of memories, reviewing those colorful and sonorous exchanges, and lamenting the present

---

1 ~~Li Yong and Tian Zh~~onghe, "Discovering Value and Beauty in the Dilemma of Humanity: An Interview with Tian Zhonghe", Fiction Review, No. 2, 2012.

and the past. with grief over the fall of the past dynasties. The tone of the narrative is smooth and soothing, friendly and comfortable, a warm narrative.[1]

In March, the novel *Love in the Twentieth Century*[2] was published in the 2nd issue of *October*. In the introduction of the novel, Tian Zhonghe said: "This topic has been brewing in my mind for more than twenty years. ...... Starting from 1995, I wrote 300,000 words in each chapter in a single narrative style on an experimental basis, and some chapters were published in the form of medium-sized novels, but in the end I felt unsatisfied with them and put them away for a few years. I picked them up again in 2003."[3] "The characters in the novel come from my hometown, from my familiar neighbors, relatives and friends. I used to live with them and spend unforgettable years together during the world-famous turning periods in Chinese history."[4] "Father's and her" is written in an open and heavy style, which not only shows the history of China in the twentieth century through the emotional journey of an intellectual, but more importantly conveys the thoughts on Chinese national culture and national humanity through several flesh and blood characters, and unveils the heavy theme of the alteration of humanity through the symbolism of the four protagonists."[5]

Tian Zhonghe thinks that the novel is characterized by two features: "One is that it touches upon the process of alienation of the freedom of each

---

1 Miao Bianli, "The Multiple Variations of the Song of Youth and Spring - A Study of Tian Zhonghe's Growth Narrative of Seventeen", Nanfang Literature Forum, No. 4, 2012.

2 In August 2010, the novel was renamed Father and Them when it was published by Writer's Publishing House.

3 Mo Bai and Tian Zhonghe: Dialogue with Mo Bai: The Spiritual World of Novels, in Tian Zhonghe Prose Essays, Lost in My Own Heart, Henan University Press, 2012, p. 487.

4 Tian Zhonghe: "Two Notes on the Creation of 'Father and Them,'" in Tian Zhonghe's Essays and Prose: Lost Within Oneself, Henan University Press, 2012, p. 479.

5 Mo Bai and Tian Zhonghe, "Dialogue with Mo Bai: The Spiritual World of Novels", in Tian Zhonghe Prose Essays, Lost in Their Own Minds, Henan University Press, 2012, p. 483.

and every individual of this people, a theme which has not been touched upon in our literature so far. This is its ideological value. Another is its exploration in art, the structure of this long novel is unprecedented, with double postulates, polyphony, and multi-angle. These two points are the value of the existence of this novel."[1]

Other major works published in this year include: Creative Talk: "The Spiritual World of Fiction - Dialogue on Tian Zhonghe's New Novel Father and Them" (Mo Bai and Tian Zhonghe, *Literature Newspaper*, October, No.14), Interview: "When We Get Old, When We Talk About Love - Interview with Lu Jing" (*Chinese Literature*, Issue 8), Creative Talk: "How Slavery is Made" (*Selected Long Stories*, Issue 6).

2011, 71 years old

In March, the novel *Seventeen* was published by Jiangsu Literary Arts Publishing House.

Research papers on Tian Zhonghe in that year include: Liu Jun, "Burden of Concealment and Self-abridgement: Two Mothers in 'Father and Them'", *Journal of Zhengzhou University* (Philosophy and Social Science Edition), No.1; Miao Bianli, "Telling and Reflecting on 'Father and Them'", *Yangzijiang Review*, No.1; Zhang Zhouzi, "A Complex Dialogue among Tradition, Modernity and Revolutionary Culture", *Journal of Pingdingshan University*, No.3; Li Shaorong, "Traumatic Memories of Modern Intellectuals and the Meaning of Trauma in '*Father and Them*'", *Journal of PingdingshanUniversity*, No.3;

Wang Chunlin, "Intellectuals, Revolution, and Twentieth-Century Chinese History: A Review of Tian Zhonghe's Long Novel, Father and Them", *Journal of Pingdingshan University*, No. 3; Lin Hong and Hu Hongchun,

1 Miao Meiling and Tian Zhonghe, "Walking Freely in the Literary Scene: An Interview with Tian Zhonghe," *Dongjing Literature*, No. 3, 2012.

"History-Love-Humanity: A Review of Tian Zhonghe's New Novel, 'Father and Them'", *Literary and Cultural Controversy*, No. 9; Liu Jun, "*Seventeen*: A Personal Slice of the Past and a Reduction of History", *Yangzijiang Review*, No. 4; Liu Siqian, "This One" and "the Other" in Tian Zhonghe's "Two Mother" Characters in his Long Novel 'Father and Them'", *Zhongzhou XueKan*, No. 6.

2012, 72 years old

The novel "*Father and Them*" won the first Dufu Literature Prize. The collection of essays "Lost in My Own Heart" was published by Henan University Press.

Other major works published in this year include: Creative Talks: How Am I Living in the 21st Century? (*Fiction Review*, No.2), Dialogue "Discovering Value and Beauty in the Dilemma of Humanity - An Interview with Tian Zhonghe" (Li Yong and Tian Zhonghe, No.2, *Fiction Review*), Short Story "The Death of a Carpenter" (*Dongjing Literature*, No.3), Creation Dialogue "Candlelight of Humanity to Illuminate the History - After the Death of a Carpenter" (*Da Guan*, No. 3), Dialogue 'Walking Freely in the Scene of Literature - An Interview with Tian Zhonghe' (Miao Meiling, Tian Zhonghe, *Daguan*, No.3), and Creative Talks 'Re-reading 'May'' (*Tonight Newspaper*, April 19th).

The main research papers on Tian Zhonghe in that year include: Huang Yi, "Identity: The Twentieth Century Chinese Knot", *Fiction Review*, No. 2; Li Yong, "The Woes of the Thinker and the Ease of the Artist: On Tian Zhonghe's Novel Creation", *Fiction Review*, No.2; Mi Xuejun, "Another Ode to Mother's Love", *Fiction Review*, No. 2; Miao Bianli, "The Multiple Variations of 'The Song of Youth': A Study of the Coming-of-Age Narrative in Tian Zhonghe's 'Seventeen', *Southern Literature Forum*, No.4; Zhou Limin, "Grass Seedlings on the Ground", *Nanfang Literature Forum*, No.5;

Liu Si-Qian, "Narrative Mode and Characterization of Father and Them", *Nanfang Literature Forum*, No. 5; Fang Wei, "Reflection on History and Artistic Innovation", *Nanfang Literature Forum*, No. 5; Huo Junming, "His Continuing Song of Love", No. 1, *Nanfang Literature Forum*; Huo Junming, "He is a Continuous Minority: Tian Zhonghe's Recent Works and the Difficulty of 'Contemporary' Writing", *Nanfang Literature Forum*, No. 5; Liu Hongzhi, "The Writer's Self-consciousness of Thought and Art - Talking about Tian Zhonghe's Recent Works", *Nanfang Literature Forum*, No. 5; Liu Hongzhi, "Transmutation of Words and Transformation of Revolutionary Narrative: The Breakthrough of Tian Zhonghe's 'Fathers and Them' to the Traditional Revolutionary Narrative," *Zhengzhou University Journal* (Philosophy and Social Science Edition), No. 6.

2014, 74 years old

In June, a collection of short and medium-sized stories, *Tomorrow's Sun*, was published by Henan People's Publishing House. This collection of short stories is one of the series of famous old writers and artists in Henan Province compiled by the Federation of Literary and Art Circles of Henan Province.

2015, 75 years old

In January, the novella "Kulkara Love" and its creation talk "Kaleidoscope of Humanity" were published in the first issue of *Daguan* (Dongjing Literature)".

"Kulkara Love is an excerpt from his forthcoming novel, a novel with autobiographical meaning, in which the hero is based on his second brother who worked in Xinjiang farms, and describes the life of intellectuals in a special era, which is a heartfelt work that has been brewing for many years."[1]

---

1 Zhang Yanwen, "The Voice of the Lost Speaker - Review of Tian Zhonghe's 'Kulkara Love'", Da Guan (Dongjing Literature), No. 1, 2015.

In April, "Tian Zhonghe Studies"[1] edited by Xu Hongjun was published by Hennan University Publishing House, which is the first historical compilation showing the results of Tian Zhonghe studies, "It is a collection of Tian Zhonghe's autobiographies, 5 articles of creative writing, 2 articles of literary dialogues, 2 articles of interviews, 2 articles of impressions, 28 articles of research theses, 1 article of chronology of his works, and 1 article of index of his research materials." [2]

The main research papers on Tian Zhonghe in that year include: Li Yong, "The Way of Recounting History", *Daguan* (Dongjing Literature), No.1; Liu Haiyan, "Non-mainstream Writer: Tian Zhonghe", *Daguan* (Dongjing Literature), No.1; Zhang Yanwen, "The Voice of the Lost Speaker: A Review of Tian Zhonghe's "Kulkara Love"", *Daguan* (Dongjing Literature), No.1; Li Xiao-zheng, "Historical Telling: Reliable and Unreliable: On the Paradoxical Character of the Narrator in 'Father and Them'", *Journal of Zhengzhou University* (Philosophy and Social Science Edition), No.4;

Guo Haobo, "Emasculated Subject: On the Literary Historical Significance of Tian Zhonghe's Character Image in his Long Story 'Father and Them'", *Shanhua*, No. 20; Zhu Ling, "The Earth - Mother's Love- Poetic Sentiment, An Analysis of the Thematic Imagery in the Ecological World of Tian Zhonghe's Countryside", *Literature Review Series of Chinese Modern Literature*, No. 2.

1 This book is one of the series of research materials on the writers of the Central Plains edited by Cheng Guangwei and Wu Shenggang, the others being: Bai Hua Study, February River Study, Li Er Study, Li Peifu Study, Liu Qingbang Study, Liu Zhenyun Study, Mo Bai Study, Shao Li, Qiao Ye, Ji Wenjun Study, Yan Lianke Study, Zhang Yigong Study, Zhang Yu Study, and Zhou Daxin Study.
2 Xu Hongjun: "Tian Zhonghe Studies - Afterword", in Tian Zhonghe Studies, Henan University Press, 2015, p. 259.

The "Fading" Countryside and the "Blurred" City - A Side of Henan Short Stories and Novellas in 2017

The year 2017 is a noteworthy year for novel creation in Henan. This year, Henan writers published seven novels, namely Li Peifu's *Plains Guest* (Hua Cheng, Issue 3, Hua Cheng Publishing House), Qiao Ye's *The Story of the Hidden Pearl* (October-Long Stories, Issue 3, Writers Publishing House), Liang Hong's *Liang Guangzheng's Glorious Dreams* (Contemporary, Issue 5, People's Literature Publishing House renamed it as *Liang Guangzheng's Light*), Liu Zhenyun's S*ons and Daughters in the Age of Gossips* (Yangtze River Literature and Arts Publishing House), Tian Zhonghe's *Blurred* (Chinese Writers, Issue 12, renamed Tagadaria Reeds by Writer's Press in 2018), Zong Pu's *The Book of Returning to North China* (People's Literature, No. 12) and so on. Some scholars did a survey of 35 novel ranking lists in 2017, and among the top 21 long novels, the novels written by Henan writers are very popular. Among them, *Liang Guangzheng's Light*, *The Plain Guest* and *Sons and Daughters in the Age of Gossip* ranked the top. [1]

As in the case of long novels, short and medium-sized novels have also performed well, with excellent works by writers of the elder, middle-aged and young generations, including Liu Qingbang's *The Cow*, *Is There a Ghost or Not*, *Ying's Four Acts*, *Swallows Pick Up the Mud to Mei's House*, *Red Cotton Jacket*, *Leave Me Alone*, *Love of Pants* and so on, published in important literary journals such as Comtemporary, Shanghai Literature, Fiction Bimonthly Journal, and *The Cow* was also awarded the "Annual Short and Medium-Sized Fiction Champion" of the Contemporary in 2017. Shao Li, Qiao Ye and Ji Wenjun published *The River*, *The Summer of Li Xia*, *The Artistic Life of Jiang Jinlu*, *A Brief History of Forty-Three Years*, *Zero-Zero-*

1 He Ping, "In the era of 'ranking', literature that pretends to be noticed", South Weekend, March 31, 2018.

One Millimeter, *Go to Jail* and *The City of Hua* in publications such as Beijing Literature, Writers, Contemporary, People's Literature, Works and Guangxi Literature and other publications. Young writers Nan Feiyan and Li Qingyuan published *Leather Wedding*, *Red Dust Puffing*, *Nothing to Do with the Wind and the Moon*, and *The Stubborn Resident on ZuntiAn Street* in publications such as People's Literature and October, which made a deep impression on the audience. Post-90s writer Zheng Zaihuan has published a collection of short stories called *A Collection of Heartbreaking Stories from Zumadian* in Shanghai Literary Arts Publishing House and published *What's Outside*, *There are Ghosts in the World*, *Getting a Head Start* and other short stories in People's Literature and other publications, making him one of the "Post-90s" Henan writers who have attracted a great deal of attention in the past two years, along with Wang Su Xin and Zhi Ah Wei, etc.

I. The Distortion of Experience and the "Fading" of the Countryside

In contemporary Henan literature, novels are far more popular than poems, songs, essays, plays and other genres. The contemporary Henan writers who are well known in the country are almost all novelists: Yao Xueyin, Li Zhun, Liu Zhenyun, Zhou Daxin, Li Peifu, Li Er, and Er Yuehe ...... Among the novels, the novels with rural themes are absolutely dominant: *Can't Go That Way, Li Shuangshuang, The Yellow River Flows East, Yellow Flowers of the World in the Hometown, A word is worth a thousand words, Year, Month and Day, Daylight, Bombing, Lake and Mountain, The Door of the Sheep, The Book of Life, Cherry Peaches on the Pomegranate Tree,* and so on. These novels, which have shone so brightly in the history of contemporary Chinese literature, are all written about the rural areas of Henan Province. From this, we can basically come to the conclusion that the contemporary literature of Henan is, to a large extent, characterized by the creation of novels on rural themes. The emergence of this phenomenon is closely related to the social and economic development of Henan. As the granary of China, Henan has always gained the main force of its economic development from agriculture, and most of its population is mainly concentrated in the countryside. Agriculture, rural villages and farmers have always played an important role in the socio-economic development of Henan. Therefore, the main content of Henan literature naturally shows more rural themes.

However, things are changing. For one thing, with the deepening of urbanization in Henan, the impact of cities on the country's socio-economic, cultural and living conditions is gradually increasing. According to the "2017 National Economic and Social Development Statistics Bulletin of Henan Province" jointly released by Henan Provincial Bureau of Statistics and Henan Survey Team of National Bureau of Statistics on February 28, 2018, in 2017, "the urbanization rate of the permanent population in Henan Province exceeded 50 percent for the first time, reaching 50.16 percent."[1] On the other hand, the composition of contemporary writers in Henan is also changing quietly, and a group of writers who have grown up and lived in the cities are becoming the vital force of contemporary literature in Henan. The combination of these two factors is gradually changing the overall face of contemporary Henan literature.

Among the short stories written in Henan in 2017, only Liu Qingbang and Zheng Zaihuan seem to be the only writers who have really written about the countryside and made a big impact. Liu Qingbang is famous for his short stories, and his rural novels about the plains of eastern Henan have become a typical representative of contemporary Chinese rural novels, and his novels such as *Shoes*, *Mei Niu Sheep-herding*, *Rattles* and *Gold Scattered* have entered various anthologies of short stories and have become the classic pieces of contemporary Chinese rural writing. However, when we carefully read his

1 https://www. henan. gov. cn/2018/02-28/387734. html.

short stories written in 2017, we will find that his writing about the countryside seems to be gradually departing from the current rural reality. On the surface, *The Cow* and *Red Cotton Jacket* seem to be written at the present time, but when we scrutinize the logic of the development of the stories and the atmosphere of the novels, we can realize that these stories took place at least in the 1990s. *The Cow* is about the changing emotions of farmers in rural life, and it has been commented that "against the background of rapid urbanization, Liu Qingbang's exploration of rural themes in the novel embodies the power of realist writers to express reality through literature".[1]In my opinion, this kind of evaluation is more or less full of praise. From the point of view of the exploration and expression of real life, this novel does not exceed Liu Qingbang's previous works of rural fiction, and compared with those novels, it can even be said that it still has a serious flaw, that is, the reality it writes about and the reality it wants to express are not united. On the surface, the novel is about the present, but in terms of the details and the overall atmosphere, the "lives" in the novel are not contemporary; they are at least from the 1990s of the 20th century or even earlier. For example, Hu Qidong, the main character of the novel, buys a cow at the market for 800 yuan, and as the village secretary, he raises chickens, ducks, geese, pigs, cows and goats at home, and his wife cooks pots with firewood. These details or scenes in the novel are not so much the author's "realism" of the current rural life, but rather they reveal the author's detachment from the current rural reality as well as his deep impression of the rural life in his own memories, which is hard to be shaken. Judging from the price of cows, the story in the novel happened at least 20 years ago; judging from the lifestyle of the yard full of chickens and ducks, the rural village in the author's mind may still be

---

1 "Contemporary" 2017 "Annual Short and Middle-Grade Fiction Overall Winner" Award Ceremony.

the same as it was in the 1970s and 1980s. This situation is also reflected in the novel *The Red Cotton Jacket*.

The themes expressed in these four novels, *Is There a Ghost or Not*, *Ying's Four Acts*, *Swallows Pick Up the Mud to Mei's House*, *Love of Pants*, are those of the rural areas of the present: one being the decline of the traditional culture, and the other being the life of the elderly in the rural areas. *Ying's Four Acts* takes Yu opera "Qin Xianglian" as a clue, and recounts the different ways that three generations of the Song Jinghui family deal with extramarital affairs. When his father Song Guocheng was about to fall into an extramarital affair, Song Jinghui's mother asked her son to write a letter to warn him using the story of Qin Xianglian and Chen Shimei and thus saved their marriage. Similarly, when Song Jinghui had an extramarital affair his father also used the story of Qin Xianglian to persuade him to change his mind. However, when he discovered his son Song Yang was keeping a lover, the story of Qin Xianglian couldn't even work—let alone the fact that his son did not even know who Qin Xianglian and Chen Shimei were! Let's not discuss how long such a theme has existed in contemporary literature for now. Simply from the author's depiction of the scenes from Song Jinghui's adolescence—when he listened to and performed in plays—it is clear that the rural area he is familiar with is not the one of the present day. Although *Love of Trousers* is about the morbid "love of pants" of an old man who was seriously disturbed by the problem of clothing in his youth, it is obvious that the old man's recollection of the lack of clothing in his youth is the core of the novel and also the most touching part of the novel, both from the length of the novel and from the content.

Formally, Liu Qingbang's local novels of the East Yu Plain have a prominent feature. His novels do not come up into the story, but first write the local customs, cultural traditions, and then slowly unfold the story. For example, in *Rattles*, "when someone dies in the village, it is customary to invite a band to play. They don't play when someone is born or when a bride is married, they only blow to publicize the death". In *Pulling Nets*, "In our area, there are many types of fishing nets, including cast nets, lift nets, trap nets, sticky nets, scoop nets, haul nets, drag nets, and a unique type called a sleeve net. The sleeve net is unique to our hometown, and without a brief explanation, it would be difficult for people from other areas to understand. The sleeve net…" In *Pond*, "the pond of fish all at once to catch out, the people here say is to start the pond. The day of starting the pond is the festival of the people and the last day of the fish. In *The Little Boat*, "In those years, there were many beggars, and when they couldn't finish a meal, several beggars would come to the door to beg.

The tools for begging are almost the same, all three sets, a broken bamboo basket, a tiled bowl, and a dog-beating stick". In *The Family Matchmaking*, "The family matchmaking is the first step before the marriage, and these are two procedures that cannot be reversed. The marriage must be conducted by the daughter's family themselves, and no one can take the place of. It is not the same case for matchmaking, either the daughter's father or her mother can go". In *Visiting New Guests*, "There is an unwritten rule in this place that newly married grooms must visit their bride's family on the second day of the first lunar month in their first year of marriage. The groom during this period is referred to as a 'new guest.' The process of visiting relatives on the second day of the first lunar month is referred to as 'visiting new guests". In *All the Gold Gone*, "We call the disabled people there as "talented bad guys", the blind, the lame, the deaf, are all talented bad guys, and the mute is also. Literally, the basic talent of a certain aspect of a person is broken and can't function, probably even if it's a talent bad guy". 2017 short stories also have this kind of writing, such as "Cow", the beginning of the novel is, "Maybe it's because of the deep culture of the Ya (Highbrow culture), the people of the place are a little bit awkward in their speech, and they don't want to speak too plainly. They seem to avoid words like male and female. For example, they don't refer to a ram as a ram, or as a taw-hu; nor do they refer to a ewe as a mother sheep, or as a water goat. Similarly, they do not refer to bulls as bulls, downer cows, bullocks (castrated bulls); also, they do not call the cow mother cow, but called the cow Shouniu". In *Red Cotton jacket*, "Autumn has come, the weather is cooler, the rushes are white, the leaves are yellow, and you can no longer see the geese flying south. When we were working on the collective farm, so many wild geese would appear out of nowhere. One flock after another would fly across the sky, a continuous procession overhead. The members of the production team worked in groups in the fields, and when the geese flew by in the sky, they would inevitably look up at the geese to have a look".

Through this kind of beginning, it seems that the writer can easily enter into a kind of nostalgic mood, enter into the time he wants to write about, and enter into the scene at that time. To put it simply, this kind of beginning is often the writer's brewing mood for the whole novel. For the reader, this kind of beginning is not only a buffer before we enter the story, but also an atmosphere for us to understand the story: the atmosphere of the time and the atmosphere of the environment. If our understanding is generally correct, then Liu Qingbang's 2017 novels reflecting rural realities are misplaced. The intention seems to be to reflect the present, but the memories, the atmosphere and even the logic of the whole story are still stuck in the 1970s and 1980s of the 20th century.

It is inevitable that writers of the older generation who came out of the countryside have become increasingly detached from rural life. In today's cultural context, it is unlikely that these writers will be able to go to the countryside to "live in the countryside" as the writers of the Seventeen Years period did, so they will either continue to write about the countryside in their memories, or they will turn their attention to the city. In the former area, Liu

Qingbang has been very successful, and many of these works have become his representative works. However, in the latter field, that is, in urban writing, Liu Qingbang has made some attempts, such as the "Nanny in Beijing Series", a group of works that express "life in Beijing and life in the city", as if they were trying to "enter the inner city"[1], even they do not seem to be successful. In this way, Liu Qingbang's works seem to have been unable to go beyond his memory of the Plain of East Henan and His writing cannot transcend the coal mining life he once experienced.

Compared with Liu Qingbang's writing about the current rural areas, the Henan countryside depicted by Zheng Zai-huan may be more representative of the spirit of the present day: progress and cruelty coexist, prosperity and decadence go hand in hand, noise and indifference dance together, and construction and destruction follow one another. Whether it is his *Biography of a Patient* or his more representative "Cult Family", they all contain the above spiritual qualities to different degrees. Throughout the book, *A Collection of Heartbreaking Stories from Zhumadian* is woven in a non-fictional tone of childhood memories. From the perspective of a young man, Zheng Zaihuan writes of an 'original evil', of the natural cruelty of the world and of the simple suffering of the people."[2] However, we cannot say that Zheng Zaihuan's rural village is a basic portrayal of today's rural areas in Henan. Perhaps because of his special life experience and the short period of time he has been working on his works, Zheng Zaihuan's description of rural villages in Henan more often reflects the bottom, the margins and the cruelty of the countryside, which is a part of the reality of the countryside nowadays, but far from the whole picture of the countryside. Moreover, it seems that they

---

1 Liu Qingbang, Can't Find the North: Nanny in Beijing, Beijing October Literary Publishing House, 2014, p. 1.

2 Li Zhuang: "Uncontrolled Discourse and the Loneliness of the Weak - Taking the Novel Works of A Yi, Zhao Zhiming, and Zheng Zaihuan as Examples", Southern Literature Forum, No. 2, 2018.

are also separated from nowadays, and it seems that a kind of cruelty and absurdity of the countryside was more common in the rural areas of Henan at the end of the twentieth century. Especially his "Cult Family" can be said to be unique among contemporary Chinese family novels. We have seldom seen anyone write about a family's relatives in such an unfortunate way, so brutal, so morbid, so hopeless. If Ba Jin, Cao Yu and Zhang Ailing's writing on the pathology of the family is a symbol of the decline and decay of the feudal family during the transformation of Chinese society, Zheng Zaihuan's writing on the pathology of the family can be regarded as a kind of revelation. It reveals that the rapid development of the market economy in the 1990s has brought a huge negative impact on human ethical relations in rural China. The "grandparents" raised four sons, but ended up in a miserable old age. The violent "stepmother" not only had no sense of responsibility toward her husband's parents (the grandparents) and her stepchildren, but also beat and scolded them depending on her mood. Because of my mother's death, "I" in this world has become a burden, not welcomed by any relatives. "Grandpa set himself as a role model and made all kinds of life plans for his descendants. But none of his children were able to become successful. The "younger brother, third uncle, stepmother's second brother and fourth uncle" were either violent and aggressive, or addicted to alcohol, or indulge in drinking, gambling, and prostitution, or are devoid of humanity, engaging in fighting, excessive drinking, gambling, theft, prostitution, deception, and even insulting and beating their parents—they commit every imaginable evil. Perhaps there is something humane in those family members' life stories, but they undoubtedly lived against the background of the 1990s.

The situation in Henan literature, which is famous for novels on rural subjects, is that there are fewer and fewer writings about the countryside, especially about the social reality of the countryside nowadays. It seems that this phenomenon is not unique to Henan literature; in fact, it is probably true of contemporary Chinese literary creation as a whole. This reflects at least three problems: one is that China's social structure is indeed undergoing fundamental changes, and the proportion of rural areas in the life of the whole society is gradually decreasing, which is an indisputable fact and a welcome change. The second is that the overall composition of China's writers' team is also undergoing great changes, and a large number of writers who were born, grew up, and lived in cities are becoming the vital force of Chinese writers. This change does not give me the same optimistic feeling as the prior one dose.

This is because the change of the writers' team reflects not only the change of the writers' growing environment and cultural background, but also the change of the cultural leadership. A small part of the writers who grew up in the cities may have come from rural areas, but more of them may have been born and grown up in the cities. When writers from the cities gradually became the main force of China's writers, the cultural leadership of Chinese society was transferred from writers born in the countryside to writers from the cities. This transfer of cultural leadership is probably a historical necessity, and there is nothing to be sad about. However, what is worrying is that the transfer of cultural leadership is likely to bring about the complete withdrawal of rural areas from the process of Chinese literature and Chinese cultural production. Let's not say whether Chinese literature with only urban themes is healthy or not, but the development of Chinese literature is definitely unhealthy if the problems faced by the Chinese countryside in the process of modernization no longer attract Chinese writers' attention. When the old generation of writers who came out from the countryside are gradually leaving the present rural reality, when writers who were born, grew up and lived in the cities are unable to pay attention to the present rural life, and when the countryside itself is unable to cultivate a team of writers who can express themselves, then who else is willing to express China's countryside?

The third question concerns the life resources of writers. The topic of "in-depth living" is no longer mentioned, but it is obvious that many writers who have gradually adapted to the comfortable life of the bookstore are generally facing the dilemma of depletion of writing resources. Young writers prefer to use their own lives as a backdrop for their literary creation, and many are unable to break through the narrowness of their subjects. The older generation of writers also have to collect material from various media, and the resultant works are regarded by critics as a mere collage of online news and postings.

Under such a literary environment, who would go into the countryside to express the current rural society? It is probably for this reason that People's Literature started the column "Non-fiction Writing", as an effort to guide writers to go deeper into reality. Perhaps it is also for this reason that Liang Hong's *China in Liangzhuang* and *The Record of Leaving Liangzhuang* caused a great uproar in the literary and cultural circles.

II. Women's growth and the absence of the city

Compared with the development of national literature, the problem of literature in Henan may be even more serious. Not only is rural life gradually "disappearing" from literature, but the real city life has not yet grown up in literature, and the cities in the writings of Henan writers are still basically "blurred". There are four main reasons for this: one is that Henan has not yet seen any metropolis like Beijing, Shanghai, Nanjing, and Wuhan, which have both a strong modern urban atmosphere and a more prominent urban cultural tradition. Another reason for this is that Henan writers' understanding of urban life may not be deep enough, and within a short period of time, there is no way for any city in Henan to compete with Shanghai under the pens of Mao Dun, Zhang Eileen and Wang Anyi, with Beijing under the pens of Lao She and Liu Xinwu, or with Wuhan under the pens of Chi Li and Fang Fang. The third reason is probably related to the literary tradition of Henan. So far, the mainstream of literature in Henan is still realism, and modernist literary works are still a minority. However, "Throughout the history of new literature, urban literature has always been entangled with modernism or modernism ...this does not mean that the city is a byproduct of modernism or modernist consciousness.

On the contrary, the essence of urban literature is the modern logic itself"[1] The last reason is that even when they do write about the city, Henan writers seldom express the daily life of the city, either because they want to capitalize on their strengths or because they have something else in mind.

In the short stories of Henan in 2017, three female writers, Shao Li, Qiao Ye and Ji Wenjun, splashed more ink on the urban population. In the contemporary Chinese writers' team, Henan writers have a lot of talent, almost half of the country, but there are fewer female writers, especially female novelists. Shao Li, Qiao Ye, and Ji Wenjun can be said to be the outstanding representatives of them. Perhaps there is a closer cultural affinity between women and the city. Almost all of the novels written by these three female writers in 2017 are set in the city, what's more, those works are all about the growth of urban women.

Among Shao Li's two novels about women in the city, *The River* is more famous, but in terms of artistic integrity, *Li Xia's Summer* seems to be better. The theme of *The River* is a bit confusing. In the creation talk, Shao Li explained the theme of the novel as the relationship between mother-in-law and daughter-in-law, "For a long time, I have been wanting to write about the relationship between mother-in-law and daughter-in-law"[2]. The novel consists of twelve sections, nine of which are about the mother-in-law, but in the tenth section, the novel takes a sharp turn from a description of the mother-

1 Li Danmeng, "What exactly is urban literature", People's Daily, May 26, 2015.
2 Shao Li: "About my mother-in-law - 'Big River' creation talk", http://www. sohu. com/ a/224559684_202823.

in-law and the relationship to the husband's infidelity, which inevitably makes people wonder what happened to her.

The Mother-in-law is a traditional rural woman and she has not been her husband's pleasure. The couple has been in a cold war to each other. Therefore, after the death of the father-in-law, the mother-in-law explained to the children that she would never be buried with her husband after her death. Although in marriage, the mother-in-law is an insulted and damaged woman, in family life, the mother's relationship with her son and daughter, especially the mother daughter relationship, is particularly strong, overbearing, and even beyond reasonable. Compared to her mother-in-law, "I" in the novel is portrayed as a restrained, yielding, and self-sacrificing intellectual woman who even comes across as somewhat weak, but ultimately ends up being betrayed by her husband. Therefore, by depicting the relationship between "I" and my mother-in-law, this novel aims to write about women's destiny, women's happiness and women's quality of life. Of course, the most important thing in the middle of this is the relationship between husband and wife and between mother-in-law and daughter-in-law.

Li Xia's Summer is a typical women's text, which deals with many important issues often dealt with in women's literature in the structure of a short novel: growth, trauma, love, friendship, affection, marriage, childbirth, etc. From childhood to adulthood, Xiao Xia, as a woman, has been hurt by her parents, grandmother, grandparents, stepmother, stepdaughter, and her boyfriend. From childhood to adulthood, Xiaoxia, as a woman, has been hurt by her parents, her grandmother, her grandparents, her stepmother, her stepmother's daughter and her boyfriend, all of whom are close to her, and this is a novel about trauma. However, after being seriously injured, Xiaoxia is still strong and sunny; she doesn't need a man to take care of her unborn daughter and her paralyzed mother. So, this is another novel about growing up. In addition, it is also a typical female novel, not only because its main character Li Xiaoxia is a woman, but also because its ending almost tells us this "truth": men can't be relied on, no matter fathers or boyfriends, in the process of women's growth, the ones who can be relied on seem to be more worth cherishing. In the end, it's still their own relatives, and among them are mainly mothers and daughters. But what is paradoxical is that in her early years of growing up, it was not only men who caused her harm, but also her mother, her paternal grandmother, her maternal grandmother, her stepmother and stepmother's daughter, who seemed to have caused Xiao Xia no less harm than men.

In 2017, The most readable short stories published by Qiao Ye is *Zero Point Zero One Millimeter*, *Go to Jail* and *A Brief History of Forty-three Years*, these three novels involved in the subject matter is also all urban women, of which, the most stunning is *Zero Point Zero One Millimeter*. The step-by-step approach of the human nature torture, the narrative structure of the methodical, the details of the meticulous examination, the psychological description of the appropriate depth, all of this is enough to make this short story an important harvest of Henan Literature in 2017. I don't know whether the author had considered that the heroine of the novel and the narrator behind her were interrogating China's patriarchal ideology and traditional concepts when she created the novel, but they also unintentionally exposed the bias or even aberration in the ideology and psychology of some feminists. If we only take this novel as an example, we can see that it is a very important part of the story of a woman's life. If we only regard this novel as a women's novel criticizing men's rights, we may have seriously underestimated its value. It is not merely a critique of patriarchy; rather, it is also a reflection on feminism. Its deeper objective is directed toward humanity—humanity without distinction of gender. In realizing this great goal, the author uses psychological descriptions, details and narrative techniques. Generally speaking, because of the length of the novel, it is difficult to have a very complicated psychological description in a short novel, but the psychological description in this novel is quite successful.

The psychological preparation of the heroine when she was sexually abused by the driver, and the complexity of her sexual relationship with the driver are both deep, twisted and truly touching. In the development of the story and characterization, the details of the novel play a crucial role, and this ability to elaborate on details is a great test of the writer's skills.

Go to Jail is about a friendship between Liu Yu, a female editor of a publishing house, and Chang He, a local official. When it comes to the relationship between a young woman and an official, we often feel that it is not clean, and that there is something fishy going on. However, the friendship between Liu Yu and Chang He was as pure as water. This is a different mood. Chang He, on the other hand, went to jail. Since he got in, he must be unclean, but judging from the novel, he is not a vicious and corrupt official. He has suffered from poverty since he was a child, but he has grown up to be filial to his mother, and he has a clearer understanding of the ways of officials, and he also has some literary sentiment. This is another mood. It breaks our general image of corrupt officials. In fact, this is also a kind of human nature, a kind of quite normal, or more normal human nature. The strength of this novel lies in the fact that it is written in an unhurried and unhurried manner, without moving, but with a different mood. So, it can get the 2017 Guangxi literature award is also considered to be deserved.

A Brief History of Forty-Three Years was not only published in the national magazine People's Literature, but also reprinted in the Novel Monthly, which made the author, Qiao Ye feel surprised, since he thought this novel was not popular. [1] However, compared with the first two stories, A Brief History of Forty-Three Years is somewhat inferior. It writes a woman's 43-year

1 Qiao Ye's microblog on January 22, 2018 .

life story in 13 separate and closely related sections, including friendship, love, affection, studies, work, life, and death. Its expression of life is a bit like Liu Zhenyun's "Chicken Feathers on the Ground" and Ji Li's "Not Talking about Love", and if we look for a place for it in the history of literature, it can probably be categorized into the spectrum of the "new realism". The difference is that it has obvious feminist colors. In "her" life, the most important people are her grandmother, her parents and her daughter; the others seem not to be worth trusting and not so important to her, including her husband, her brothers, and former lovers. The unsatisfactory part of this novel is that its description is too rough; thus a lot of the content in it has been skimmed over by the rough plotline. According to its structure, it can be written into a longer work.

Hua City should be Ji Wenjun's most important work in 2017, and it was very popular after its publication, being reprinted in many literary journals. Like the novels of Shao Li and Qiao Ye, it focuses on the growth and fate of women. Born in a rural village in Henan Province, Jiang Lili was "sold by her biological parents two days after her birth, abused by her adoptive parents in the same year, and sexually abused by a teacher in middle school. She paid her way through college, and was beaten up for being a 'mistress'. Her writing was not accepted because she was blamed for being 'lack of life'. Her fiancé's voice 'run away' made Beijing her sad city ...... " She formed a deep friendship with her university classmate Lin Xiaoxiao, who came from a vastly different background, but their friendship was shattered when she betrayed Lin Xiaoxiao by sharing a video of her aunt Ai Wei's domestic violence. At the end of the novel, we could not see any light. All these are similar to previous women's novels, so what makes it special? From the theme, it involves the operation of multimedia. This seems to be a relatively new field in pure literary creation. Ai Wei was not only an editor of a fashion magazine, but also operates the WeChat public number, runs a WeChat store, hosts a talent show, establishes a cultural media company, and has become not only a cultural celebrity, but also a well-capitalized white-collar worker in the city. However, behind the scenes of new media operations, there are complex schemes, tricks and secret battles.

In terms of the form of the novel, Ji Wenjun is a relatively mature novelist who is likely to have great achievements in the future, which can probably be said in the following aspects: first, profound literary skills. Although it is only a novella, it is obvious that Ji Wenjun has borrowed and absorbed classical Chinese literature, especially Dream of Red Mansions, as well as foreign literature, especially modernist literature, in the atmosphere of the novel, which makes her novel both modern and classical. It is modern not only in its skillful writing of new media operations, but also in its detailed portrayal of modern urban life. Its classicism is reflected in the meticulous plotting of the protagonist's daily life on the one hand, and in the use of her highly decorative language on the other. Secondly, the language is trendy, classical, shrewd and compact. New trendy words on the Internet, such as APP, add support, tone, soft advertising, personification, genuine reasoning, HR, smacking body straight, and forcefulness, appear frequently in the novel, which On the one hand, makes the novel's language particularly trendy, and on the other hand, it affects the reading and acceptance of the novel. The novel's exquisite descriptions of the main character's clothes and food, such as "love is thick with gambling and tea, love is sad with burning flowers and musk", "a thick and soft woolen staircase carpet with a dark red background and a bright yellow floral pattern", "smiling with a light heart", "the skirt floating, the green and pink, the smile," etc., is always exuding a classical temperament. In terms of narrative, there are some storylines in which the characters (who all seem to be human beings) know each other very well, but they are not revealed, and the narrator only describes or even alludes to the understanding between the characters, but does not explain the whole story, as if to do so is to underestimate the reader's intelligence, or to disdain that - if you can't understand it, then you're too stupid. But then, readers aren't always as savvy as the narrator, or as inveterate in the machinations of the new media industry, and I'm afraid there are someone who don't understand, like me. So sometimes this shrewdness leads to a degree of ambiguity, opacity and incompleteness in the plot of a novel, which is never a good thing, and can lead to a degree of boredom on the part of the reader. The key realization is that the novel will omit some transitional or connecting words in the narrative, and directly stitch the core words together, which makes the reading slower, and may even form a certain reading impediment. When this compactness is combined with her modifying language, reading becomes more difficult. Again, the narrative structure is characterized by the interpenetration of reality and memories. The climax of the novel comes right at the beginning - Jiang Zi is scolded by Ai Wei's nephew and Jiang Zi's close friend Lin Xiaoxiao for secretly filming the video of Ai Wei suffering from domestic violence and disseminating it on the Internet, and then the author recount Jiang Zi and Lin Xiaoxiao's friendship, Jiang Zi's childhood trauma, teenage ups and downs, adult encounters, and then in the penultimate section of the novel, only to return to the first section of the narrative of the climax of the climax, the climax over, the novel is also the end. This kind of structure, loop reciprocating, interlocking, before and after, integrated, to a certain extent, the achievement of the artistic value of the novel.

Although the novels of Shao Li, Qiao Ye and Ji Wenjun are all about the life stories of women in the city, the city in these novels is only a place for the activities of the main characters, a background for the stories, and far from being an important object of expression in the novels, either because the authors' focus of attention is more on the women or because the authors lack sufficient experience in writing about the city space. The city in these novels is still only a place for the main character's activities and a background for the story, far from becoming an important object of expression. In these novels, whether it is the stories between a city in East Henan and Zhengzhou, or between Zhengzhou and Kaifeng (by Shao Li), between a small city in North Henan and Zhengzhou (by Qiao Ye), or between Zhengzhou and Beijing (by Ji Wenjun), it seems that all the stories staged are women's "two-city stories". However, no matter in which story, these cities are "blurred"; we can't see the appearance of these cities, can't feel the rhythm of these cities, and can't experience the culture of these cities. In the final analysis, these novels cannot be regarded as urban literature in the true sense.

Perhaps we are at a turning point in the development of contemporary Henan literature today. Writers of the older generation still write about Henan's countryside more in their memories of the traditional rural life. The younger generation of writers has already moved from the countryside to the city. Some of them, such as Liang Hong and Zheng Zaihuan, through ruminations on their own childhood experiences and field investigations of the current rural reality, have the ability and reason to write books such as China in Liangzhuang", "Out of Liangzhuang", "Liang Guangzheng's Light", "Zhumadian Heartbreaking Stories", and other excellent works of vernacular literature, but with the departure of the body and the mind from the countryside, it seems to be an indisputable fact that writers in Henan are gradually moving away from the present rural world. As for urban literature, Henan has not formed a strong literary tradition, and seems to lack sufficient social conditions. Perhaps Henan writers have not developed a special interest in it, and real urban literature has not yet been produced in Henan. However, "It is a sailing ship on the horizon whose masthead is already visible to those watching from the shore. It is the morning sun, its brilliant light already seen by those standing on the mountaintop, poised to burst forth. It is a restless baby in its mother's womb, about to be born."[1]. With the gradual progress of urbanization in Henan and the in-depth experience of urban cultural life by Henan writers, in the near future, urban literature in Henan can become an important part of contemporary Chinese literature, just like the vernacular literature in Henan.

1 Mao Zedong, "A single spark can start a prairie fire", in The Selected Works of Mao Zedong (Volume 1), People's Publishing House, 1991, p. 106.

Torturing Humanity with Feminism, or the Other Way Around

- On Qiao Ye's Short Story Zero Point Zero One Millimeter

Qiao Ye's short story Zero Point One Millimeter, published in 2017, is a significant achievement in short stories in recent years. Its narrative structure is organized, details are elaborated meticulously, and psychological descriptions are appropriate and deep. More importantly, it not only realizes the successful writing of women's existence within a limited space, but also expresses the revelation and reflection of Chinese female intellectuals on the problems of women themselves in a spirit of introspection that serves as a reminder. This makes it transcend the general sense of women's literature and has a universal human power.

Qiao Ye, who started her literary career with prose writing, has been making a great deal of progress and momentum in novel writing in recent years. Unlike her prose, which is so elegant and gentle, Qiao Ye's novels are shrewder and more sophisticated, thick and steady. Not only does she show a broad and deep tendency in the exploration of social themes, but she also exudes a subtle and profound style in her writing on human feelings and humanity. "Her novels about the inner growth process of female psychology have constructed a unique landscape of Chinese novels in the contemporary perspective."[1] In terms of the torture of human nature, her short story "Zero Point Zero One Millimeter" published in the first issue of Works in 2017 can be said to be an important harvest of short stories in recent years of the contemporary literary world.

The story of the novel is actually very simple. The heroine is an intellectual woman in her forties who is so tired of her marriage that she has

1 Liu Jun, "Qiao Ye's Novels: Small Narratives and Female Growth", Chinese Modern Literature Research Series, No. 12, 2014.

nothing new to offer, but she is still trying to maintain her marriage for the sake of her children. One rainy night, she buys a condom at a drugstore and takes a taxi home, where she is forced by a young driver to have sex. For her own safety, she asked the driver to use a condom. In the process of having sex, she not only developed a slight sympathy for the driver, but also a long-lost physical pleasure. When it was over, she asked the driver to take her home. When she got home, her husband became suspicious of her because of some minor irregularities. She could have gotten away with it, but she deliberately told her husband the whole story and that she had used a condom. Naturally, there is the questioning of her husband, but there is also the scrutiny of her husband's masculinity from a feminist standpoint. There is not only the resistance and criticism of Chinese feminism to the idea of male power, but also the revelation and interrogation of human nature in the course of the novel. To a certain extent, we can even say that Zero Point Zero One Millimeter has pushed our interrogation of human nature to a dead end.

I. The Approaching Torture of Human Nature

If the heroine unlocked the door in the bathroom is an unconscious action (she may subconsciously think that her behavior today is a bit shameful), then, when her husband asked her about the reason for unlocking the door, she was reluctant to give a reason, so there might be a deliberate component, she may be hoping to use this as a breakthrough to divorce with her husband. "Tonight's thing is a big hole, all depends on her needle and thread. As long as she is randomly looking for a patch to sew on, the day can also be broken old muddled to go on. But what if it's not normal? What if she just doesn't patch it? Just let him see this big hole? How will he react? How will things go on? Stepping out of the taxi and walking home, this curiosity flickered and tried to take hold, suddenly growing uncontrollably."[1]

---

1 The original works quoted in this article are all from *Works*, No.1, 2017, Qiao Ye, "Zero Point Zero One Millimeter", and will not be labeled later.

So, she chose to tell the truth. In saying this, her psychology is not aggrieved, not panic, but very calm, in her story, "time, place, person, event. Be clear and concise". At this time, the image of this woman is complex. From the disharmony and repression in the couple's life, to the resistance, acceptance, enjoyment and pity when she was raped, to the unconscious avoidance when she first came home, finally, she throws out the whole process and some of her real thoughts at that time.

Consciously or unconsciously, she kicks the ball to her husband; the novel's torture of human nature moves to the next stage: the torture of her husband and of all men. The torturers are not only female readers, but also male readers (who are also the tortured), and also the heroine, who is not pure in soul - when she reveals all her sufferings to her husband, she looks at her husband's "interrogation" of her like a judge, sensibly, calmly and even mockingly. "The more he asked, the more he showed his weakness, his hypocrisy, his chauvinism. She was like a spectator, watching her husband perform all kinds of "acts" in front of her according to her own imagination - except for one thing that slightly surprised her: at first, he decided to call the police. This decision made her feel that there was still some "blood" in him, and "kept her in a state of respect for him".

This part of the story is in fact a very brutal fight: a kind of naked display of human weakness. On the surface, it is the husband who is "interrogating" his wife, and it is the husband who is "interrogating" his wife's chastity with the traditional Chinese patriarchal ideology; but if you think about it deeper, you will find that it is actually her husband and the traditional Chinese patriarchal ideology who are "interrogated"; think it even deeper, we will also find that, what was shown is not only the weakness of Chinese men, hypocrisy and patriarchy, but also a kind of mean thoughts in modern Chinese female intellectuals' hearts: kick the ball to the man, to provoke the anger of men, watching men in front of themselves like monkeys to do all kinds of ridiculous "performances" in front of them, in order to show the ridiculous and pathetic ugly face of Chinese men.

Why am I saying this? Is it my male chauvinism? Perhaps, perhaps I am as weak and hypocritical as the husband in the novel, with a deep-rooted patriarchal mindset. But, looking at the novel itself, my assumptions are by no means conjectures. If the wife is an ordinary woman with little education, or even a very traditional and conservative Chinese woman, then, when she comes home and faces this "interrogation" from her husband, we will only think that she is innocent, that she is pitiable, and that her husband is hypocritical, weak, and patriarchal. But the heroine of the novel is not such a woman; she is an intellectual woman with a very clear feminist mindset, she is deliberately trying to provoke her husband, she wants to see how he will face the situation, and she is generally aware of what he might do - this is her complexity.

Let us look at some of her actions when her husband "interrogated" her. In the retelling of the rape, the heroine describes the "time, place, person and event. Be clear and concise." "She first sat down and looked up at him. The husband was weakly tall and looked intensely unreal." The word "looked up" here is only in its original sense, and does not carry any admiring element, but "sat down first" is quite meaningful; she sat down to look at her husband "weakly tall and looked intensely unreal," to watch his performance. In answering her husband's question, she was not flustered, almost without expression, as is clear from the words of her answer: "Slept." "A little tired." "No one around." "No." The sentences are very short and simple, ending with a period, without hesitation or unnecessary words and explanations. There is also a description of the husband's behavior: "He gets up, goes to the window, pushes it open, closes it, and pushes it open again. Then he sat back down and took his cell phone and swiped the screen one by one. His hands were so busy on the phone, his face was so busy, all his micro-expressions were stretched to the limit." Her surprising, uncanny calm contrasted with her husband's panicked, fidgety nervousness. In the face of such a situation, it is difficult for us to put ourselves in the heroine's position and criticize the man in front of her. On the contrary, we may wonder about the heroine's psychological world at this moment: what has her husband done wrong? Why should he be put in such an embarrassing situation?

In the sixth section, the novel takes a step closer to criticizing male power, which is mainly centered on three things: the use of an intrauterine device (IUD), the questioning of why the condom is worn, and the visit to the scene. Undoubtedly, these three points are fatal to the husband's critique, and he is powerless: the reason for the woman to wear the contraceptive ring is only to better satisfy her husband's sexual desire; yet, the damage it causes to the woman is left unconsoled. In contrast, the woman who accepts the driver's rape and puts a condom on him in order to minimize the damage is not understood and not forgiven. In the Chinese cultural environment, I am afraid that not many husbands can understand this kind of behavior. It is precisely for this reason that this kind of criticism is all the more powerful. The incident of going to the scene, in fact, is also a manifestation of the husband's distrust of his wife, who wonders under what circumstances such a thing could have happened. That is why the heroine thinks that the "suspect" is not the taxi driver but herself.

Another thing her husband couldn't accept was that after the rape, she came back in the car of the "suspect". This is, in any case, difficult to accept: if you do not resist, you gave him a condom in order to minimize the damage, then, after being raped, how can you still ride back in his car? The reason she gave was: "There was no other car, it was such a long way. It was raining." "Should she have walked back from the dark countryside, step by step?" This may sound like a reasonable statement, but at the end of the day, it's because she has accepted the taxi driver deep down in her heart. We have reasons to believe that if she rejected, loathed and disgusted the taxi driver from the bottom of her heart and the relationship between her and the driver, then no matter how far the road was, no matter how dark the night was, and no matter how heavy the rain was falling, she would have left the taxi driver, even if she needed to walked back home. Therefore, her reasoning is not tenable. Her husband is also understandably suspicious of her on this point, after all, the two people have not yet divorced, no husband can accept his wife actually accepting a stranger in the matter of sex. Therefore, although she feels deep in her heart that she is "alone in the wilderness", as if very aggrieved, as if she has been further abandoned, but let us think about her husband's heart and what feelings? Is this a kind of betrayal?

At night, when she went to bed, the heroine went to the bathroom twice, and when she passed by their bedroom, she noticed her husband's movements: the first time, there was no sound, so she deduced that he was thinking about the day's events, and said in a slightly mocking tone: "He is indeed thinking about it." The second time her husband snored, and She knew her husband was asleep, and she asked herself sarcastically, "Has he figured it out?" A woman who has no good feelings for her husband, has decided to divorce him, for why still care so much about what he thinks? In fact, she does not care. If she really cared, she would not have thrown the matter so hard to her husband, and with a kind of playful appreciation of the mentality of watching him in front of their "performance". The reason why she paid such attention to her husband's movements was to see how he would react to the incident. In fact, no matter how he reacted, she would not be satisfied: when she could not sleep, she would laugh at his narrow-mindedness and his patriarchal thinking; when she slept, she would feel that he was shallow, heartless, and did not even care about her. This description is not so much to criticize patriarchy, but to expose the dark psychology of the heroine.

In fact, she thought more than her husband: "She thought all night, but she didn't understand." What did she think about? It was mainly about the warm and fuzzy family life between her and her husband. Their problems were both big and small. On the large side, there was no love between them-the revolutionary mentor, Lenin, said that a marriage without love was unethical. But, to a lesser extent, aren't all couples in the world like this? So, in the couple's love life, the husband does not have a big problem. If he has problems, it probably lies in: he can't satisfy his wife in sex, and he is a bit cowardly, a bit selfish, in the ideology of some chauvinism. In addition to the sexual ability, his other weaknesses are feared to be common in many men. Therefore, it is difficult to rise to the level of human nature to make an accusation against him: cowardice and selfishness are not merely men's problems; many women also exhibit these traits. These should be common human flaws

Masculinity is indeed a very important issue, but can it be a reason for the heroine to divorce him and criticize him at the same time? I think the heroine knew very well before she got married that her husband and almost all Chinese men are patriarchal to varying degrees, and that this is a collective unconsciousness of Chinese men, and also of some Chinese women. That being the case, if her husband's patriarchal thinking is not particularly outrageous, it should not be a reason for the heroine to criticize her husband, because it is a problem of traditional Chinese culture, not a problem of any particular man. Therefore, as far as the heroine is concerned, it's not that she can't get divorced, since you are not satisfied with the sex life between husband and wife, and at the same time, you are not satisfied with this kind of loveless marriage, you can say it and get divorced. You should not put your husband into such an embarrassing situation, and take advantage of an extreme incident that you can not completely clean up to torture your husband

and see him expose his cowardice, selfishness and patriarchy in front of you, and use this as a reason to criticize him morally and humanly - this can only be said to be a kind of insidious.

In the seventh section of the fight, the heroine finds it intolerable that her husband does not care whether he can return safely or not, but focuses on the condom, valuing his wife's chastity and fidelity more than her life and safety. The heroine is disgusted by the husband's concept and his hypocritical politeness. But the aggressive posture of the heroine is at least a little uncomfortable: although the husband's ideas are questionable and need to be criticized, are you really so justified? Is your obedience, your indulgence, your wildness so flawless?

Although the words she spoke afterward were spoken in anger and without restraint, they also, to some extent, revealed her true feelings: "By asking so many questions, don't you mean that I am very cheap? Don't you mean, I am willing to be raped by him? Don't you mean that you're too bad, you can't satisfy me, so I've always been horny and horny, so I've always wanted to be raped from the bottom of my heart?!" In the first three sections of the novel, we can see very clearly that when she has sex with the taxi driver, there is indeed a desire to minimize the damage, but it also includes disappointment in her husband's sexuality, a fondness for the driver's masculinity, and enjoyment of the process of intercourse between the two of them.

The question of whether to go to the police is another sharp question. Neither the heroine nor her husband wanted to call the police. The heroine's reason for not reporting to the police was that she did not want to ruin the rest of her life with the taxi driver by reporting to the police. She thought that after reporting to the police, the driver would be arrested and she would be despised while receiving false sympathy. In this way, she seemed to be on the moral high ground. She did not report the case to the police because she did not want to ruin a young man's life on humanitarian grounds; she did not report the case to the police because she had seen through the world's ugly face and did not want to gain false sympathy and contempt from others. However, she forgot one important point: if she went to the police, she might not win. The taxi driver may not be arrested, and people may not need her humanitarian sympathy at all; likewise, because she may not win, she may not be able to gain cheap sympathy from others, and she may only receive scorn and blame. At the end of the day, her failure to report to the police is simply a matter of self-interest, yet in the narrative, she insists on cloaking themselves in moral garb.

By the same token, the husband does not report to the police, is not necessarily as she thought for being concerned that she might become a socially recognized victim after reporting to the police, and thus if the husband wants to divorce her, he will be under huge pressure and blamed morally. In fact, if her husband report to the police, she may not be able to win, or the probability of her winning is very small. In that case, her husband will discover her extramarital affair, under such public opinion conditions, what else can the husband do but divorce her? What I say doesn't mean that the husband is a good man, but I am dissatisfied with the heroine's moral stance, which always puts herself in the role of a victim and on the moral high ground, and describes everyone else as a dirty little man and a moral hypocrite. In the relationship between the heroine and the taxi driver, she can be said to be a victim; in a broader sense, in her conjugal life with her husband, she can also be regarded as a victim (after all, her husband has a patriarchal mindset), but in this case between her and the taxi driver, her husband is an innocent person - why does he become the aggressor in the conversation with her? Why is the taxi driver ignored?

According to our detailed analysis above, although this novel deals with the most secret and core issues of women, we should not simply put it into the category of women's literature. It is transcendent to women's literature in the general sense in that it not only shows a series of complicated problems that women have to face in their social and family situations, but also takes these problems as the entry point to put forward a targeted criticism of the patriarchal ideology of traditional Chinese culture; at the same time, in the process of criticizing the male culture, it also reveals and reflects on the problems of women themselves.

The point is precisely what is lacking in contemporary Chinese women's literature and even women's culture. If women do not have a clear understanding of their own problems, but only criticize male culture, or even go to the extreme of portraying themselves as a victim, standing on the moral high ground and examining male culture in an arrogant or even psychologically dark posture, the result will only be counterproductive. The result can only be counterproductive. This not only reflects that "Qiao Ye's subtle taste, detailed expression and deep search of the world of women's emotion has reached a kind of candlelight insight due to her persistence "[1], but also further shows the kind of "introspection", "self-spiritual world", which Qiao Ye has already shown in her novels in the past. It also further demonstrates the "sincerity and courage" in "introspection" and "self-spiritual world" that Qiao Ye has already shown in her previous novels. [2]

II. The Organization of the Narrative Structure

The novel is divided into 8 sections. The first section is the beginning and the origin. Without the safety set purchased by the heroine, it would have been difficult to launch the many criticisms and questions that follow. At the same time, without her tired "closed eyes", the taxi driver would not have been able to pull her to a place that was the opposite of her destination. The

1 Han Chuanxi: "Symbolic Entry into the Subtle Emotional Territory - Qiao Ye's Female Theme Novels", Literary Arts Controversy, No. 5, 2016.

2 Li Yong: "Criticism, Repentance and Action: A Comparison of Jia Pingwa's Bringing a Lamp, Qiao Ye's Confession Book and Chen Yingzhen's Mountain Road", Literary Review, No. 5, 2015.

second section is reminiscence - after the heroine gets into the taxi, she closes her eyes and remembers the past; the second section is also the——Context - these elements are the psychological basis seduce her to surrender at the time of the rape; the context is also the ongoing story itself - all the later exchanges and conflicts between her and her husband are advanced on the basis of the second section. The third section is about the rape of the heroine by the taxi driver. The fourth section is about the conversation between the heroine and the taxi driver after the rape. It not only emphasizes the naivety of the taxi driver, but also strengthens the heroine's sympathy for him, and further enriches the heroine's psychological world. The fifth section is about the conversation or psychological struggle between the heroine and her husband. This is the first round. The sixth section is about the exchanges between the heroine and her husband. Moreover, it is about the criticism of her husband. However, the darkness of the heroine's heart is also exposed in the process of criticism. This is the second round. In the seventh section, the heroine writes about three things: the heroine's memories of and boredom with the mediocre life of her husband and wife, the conflict between the husband and wife over the issue of condoms, and the exchange of views between the husband and wife over whether to call the police or not. This section can be regarded as the third round. This section can be regarded as the third round. Section eight discusses whether women should carry condoms in the face of rape. The author added this section to generalize the problems that the heroine encountered. However, there is a problem here: the husband's sexuality, his attitude towards the rapist, and the physiological experience of the rape. It is difficult for different women to agree on these issues.

From the plot review and story analysis above, we can find that the eight sections of the novel can be said to be interlocked and tightly knit. In terms of plot advancement and narrative art of the short novel, it can be said that this novel has made a lot of effort in the preparation and development of the story and the arrangement of the narrative structure.

III. The Meticulous Details of the Novel

The success of a novel cannot be separated from the meticulous and detailed description. In this regard, *Zero Point Zero One Millimeter* shows the author's extraordinary ability. Many details in the novel for the storyline of the promotion, the characterization of the role played a crucial role.

The storyline of this novel is often not driven by the narrator to complete the narrative, but by a number of particularly exquisite details. For example, the heroine after buying condoms and getting into a taxi, the driver asked her, "Where do you want to go?" Her reply was very casual: "Whatever you want." And, after saying this, "she closed her eyes". These two short dialogues not only express the fatigue and weariness of the heroine at this time, but also provide the narrative logic for the story to follow - if she had stayed alert, not rested, and watched out for the driver's route, it would have been very difficult for the rest of the story to take place.

The female protagonist's recollections are by no means random; they are a purposeful narrative. The novel gives a detail at the very beginning of the novel. "A box of ten. It's enough for a year. The last time I bought this, it must have been last year. It was also a box of ten, and I just finished using it last week." These words seem to be commonplace, but they are very important. The fact that a box of ten can last for a year is a very concise illustration of the problem that exists in their conjugal life, and it is the existence of this problem that explains the unspeakable pandering mentality of the heroine when she was raped.

It is with the reason that she just used up last week that her behavior of buying condoms is logical, and more crucially, it is because of the prop of condoms that the novel's interrogation of human nature can penetrate into the dark corners that we are unable to face.

The author seems to be worried that the detail of "a box of ten, enough for a year" does not fully rationalize the heroine's "active" acceptance of the taxi driver's sexual assault, and adds another detail - the condom is bought out of fear of accidents, abortion and suffering. She is afraid that she will have an accident and suffer from an abortion. At this point, however, the heroine develops a very strange mentality: "But now that I think about it, it was a good time to suffer from that kind of crime." This sentence seems to say that she now misses the time when she suffered from that kind of crime. Why? When her husband was fine and her sex life was harmonious. Now she doesn't have to suffer, and she doesn't have a harmonious sex life. This further rationalizes the pandering mentality she had when she was raped later.

In the course of the sexual assault, the author has described the appearance of the taxi driver in some detail. "His hair, still dripping with rain, was fresh and new. He was so young, just like a sturdy leopard." "His warm body, his strong manly odor, made her fears fade away." If we only focus our attention on the heroine, we might be puzzled by the author's meticulous description of the cab driver's appearance. However, if we take into account the psychological changes of the heroine and the development of the story, we will find that there are good reasons for the existence of such details. It is the taxi driver's youth, freshness, and warmth of his body and his strong smell of man became an important reason for the heroine to accept him in the end.

Although the heroine accepted the taxi driver, the sexual assault did not happen smoothly. "He stopped. She felt his softness. It turned out that he could not. He can't either. But he's so young." It's a particularly interesting detail that, when describing a man's sexual assault, the author paradoxically includes his physiological dysfunction. We can't help but ask: why did the author make the driver impotent at the outset? A closer look reveals that without this detail, it would have been difficult for the driver's subsequent confession to happen, and for there to be any communication and exchange between him and the female protagonist. Without this, it will reduce the heroine's good feeling and sympathy for the driver, and this sympathy and good feeling is another reason for her to accept the driver.

With all of the above: the dissatisfaction with the couple's sex life, the prediction of the serious consequences of the desperate resistance, the good feeling for the driver's fresh young male body odor, and the sympathy for the driver's life experience, the heroine has sufficient reasons for accepting the driver and even providing him with a condom - of course, among these reasons, there are both rational analysis - to minimize the harm, and desire - the lack of a rich and satisfying sex life, as well as the attraction of young males. Of course, these reasons range from rational analysis, to minimize harm, to desire, the lack of a fulfilling sex life and the attraction of young men. But all this does not mean that she is a woman who seeks only interests and physiological desires, but that she also seeks human dignity. At this point, another detail takes on special value: when the taxi driver asks the heroine if she is a prostitute, she feels "as if she had been slapped in the face. She stifled her voice: No. No.

In this case, the sexual experience with the driver brought her very complicated feelings: there are considerations of interest, there is the fulfillment of desire, but at the same time there is also the injury of human dignity.

Through the above simple combing, we can realize that the author has taken great pains to lay out all these details in preparation for the "return of all rivers to the sea" of the story. Without these details, it is difficult to understand why the heroine reacts to the taxi driver's sexual assault. Without the complex and entangled mind and action of the heroine, the dialogue and conflict between the heroine and her husband would be impossible to talk about; without this complex and wonderful life duel between the heroine and her husband, the novel's interrogation of human nature would naturally become bleak and colorless. In this sense, we can say that it is these wonderful details that make up the theme of the whole novel.

IV. The Psychological Depiction of the Novel

Logically, due to their length, short stories rarely accommodate complex psychological descriptions—but this one succeeds remarkably in this aspect. The psychological buildup leading up to the female protagonist's sexual assault by the driver—the dissatisfaction in her marriage, her consideration to minimize the harm, her attraction to the driver's masculine traits, and her sympathy for his life experiences—is gradually revealed and layered, until finally, we feel that her acceptance of the assault is inevitable and completely natural.

Her mental activities during the sexual relationship with the driver are also complex, disturbing and moving.

"At first she had an instinctive resistance." But this resistance has a component of "fear" and a component of "politeness" (she goes so far as to think that it is a kind of minimum etiquette to resist when she is being victimized, as if not resisting would not be polite enough - this kind of mentality is very special, even unthinkable, but on second thought, it is very real, even though this kind of mentality is very real. This mentality is very special, even inconceivable, but when she thinks about it, she feels that it is very real, even though it is very awkward), but there is no element of anger or shame. "As time lengthens in the senses, weak resistance soon crumbles and dissipates into silent obedience." Here, the "prolongation" is feared not only in terms of weakened physical strength, but more importantly, in terms of sexual enjoyment, and although it may seem impolite to say so, the following account confirms this idea: "In the confined space, the body temperature rises sharply, and the submissive becomes a small indulgence... Then, the indulgence blossomed wildly, and facing a strange man, she became a savage." In fact, up to here, a short story has already written the character's psychology is very subtle, but she is not finished, she is still digging down, she is analyzing the reasons for the emergence of this kind of psychology, or, the heroine is giving her own "indulgence" and "wild" to find excuses, otherwise she would have to give her own "indulgence" and "wild" to find excuses, otherwise she would have to give her own "indulgence" and "wild" to find excuses. Finding excuses, otherwise she would not be a slutty woman? She puts the blame on the condom, with which she feels that she has not lost her virginity; with which the relationship between her and the driver, though it should be described as rape, but her body's feeling tells her otherwise; with which her feeling becomes: instead of pitying herself, the driver is even more pitiful.

After the incident, the driver said to her in a consultative tone: "You will not call the police?" In the face of this question, the heroine's heart produced a series of ripples:

Of course, she should have called the police, "in the moment of the incident, this thought was the strongest". Perhaps by the time the driver drove her to the entrance of the neighborhood and drove away, her subconscious to call the police had not completely disappeared. Otherwise why would she have written down the driver's license plate number? But later, this thought "weakened, chaotically and unaccountably". In fact, it is not "chaotic" and "unclear". When we think about it carefully, there is a reason for this, and this reason exists in the analysis and interpretation of the psychological world of the heroine in our whole article.

According to some commentators, Qiao Ye's novels are always "narrated in a soft tone, every sentence and every word is a knife to the heart, unflinching, butchering the characters in her novels on the chopping board for 'fine analysis', enabling us to see the layers of muscles from skin to bone, the structure and connection of every thin capillary blood vessel and even every cell. It allows us to see the structure and connection of the characters from skin to bone, from each slender capillary blood vessel to each cell. Every time we read her novels, we feel a sense of suffocation"[1]. The excellence of this novel lies not only in the fact that it still maintains Qiao Ye's meticulous observation and subtle expression of the human condition, but also conveys a rare spirit of female introspection, which serves as a wake-up call in today's world, in addition to the excellent writing of women's encounters. This spirit not only makes the novel transcend the spiritual realm of women's literature in general, but also reaches a high standard in terms of artistic management of the novel, making it an important harvest of short story writing nowadays.

---

1 Wu Xin, "Qiao Ye :or gentle, or harsh", *Literature Free Talk*, No. 4, 2016.

Series II Literary Studies of the 1980s

Categorizing Writers' Memoirs of the 1980s - Taking New Literary Historical Materials as the Center

In recent years, the "historicization" and "disciplinization" of contemporary literature have become a remarkable academic hotspot, and the construction of historical data about contemporary literature has been increasingly emphasized by more and more scholars. In such a booming academic trend, the historical data compilation and research on the memoirs of writers in the 1980s should not be neglected. This is not only because a large number of writers' memoirs were released and published at that time, forming a prominent literary phenomenon, but also because these memoirs have been neglected in the narrative of literary history over the past thirty years and have not been subjected to basic organization and research. In order to present a more realistic and comprehensive historical overview of the literature of the 1980s, we would like to provide a preliminary basis for the study of the 1980s: to classify as exhaustively as possible the large number of writers' memoirs of the 1980s. Since these memoirs are not only numerous, but also have not yet been largely organized, therefore we would like to make a basic classification based on the New Literary History, which is the most important place for the publication of writers' memoirs in the 1980s, as well as other memoirs, in order to summarize and present the main text types of writers' memoirs in the 1980s.

I. Autobiographical Texts

(i) Autobiographies written independently by writers

1. Writers' Personal Experiences and Recounts of Creative Processes.

Authors of such memoirs generally believe that they "have lived through a multifaceted and complex life"[1] and that memoir writing can, to a certain extent, serve as a witness to history. Therefore, authors often write their memoirs with a strong sense of historical responsibility. In a broader sense, they can also be categorized as "testimonial literature". But there are some differences. One is "witnessing" in the broad sense. In this sense, all memoirs can be categorized as "testimonial literature". For example, Xia Yan's The Record of Lazy Searching for Old Dreams, Zang Kejia's Poetry and Life, Yang Hansheng's Fifty Years of Wind and Rain, and Xu Maoyong's Xu Maoyong's Recollections, etc. The other kind is "testimony" in a narrow sense. The other kind is "testimonies" in a narrower sense. They are often closely related to cultural trauma, which in contemporary Chinese history was mainly manifested during the "Anti-Rightist" and "Cultural Revolution" periods. Representative memoirs in this regard include Ba Jin's Essays, Ding Ling's The World of Snow and Wind, and Yang Jiang's Six Memoirs of the Cadre School, Chen Baichen's Broken Memories of Yunmeng, etc.

In terms of textual form, these memoirs can be categorized into series and single memoirs. The series of memoirs serialized in New Literary History include Zang Kejia's Poetry and Life, Yang Hansheng's Fifty Years of Wind and Storm, Xu Maoyong's Memoirs of Xu Maoyong, Wang Xiyan's Native Land, Years and Quest, Liang Bin's Confessions of a Novelist, Qin Mu's Memoirs of a Literary Career, Li Jiyiye's Journey of My Life, Luo Hong's Miscellaneous Memories of Creative Writing, Cao Juren's I and My

---

1 The Editorial Team of this journal: "Remembering Mao Gong's Experience of Writing Memoirs for this Journal," New Literary History, No. 3, 1981.

World, Chen Xuezhao's The Traveler Returning Home from Afar, Qin Zhao-yang's Looking Back at the Year, Xu Qinwen's Autobiography of Qinwen, Ba Ren's Travel Memoirs in Guangzhou, etc. The proportion of single memoirs is very high. The proportion of single memoirs is very large, and they can be divided into the following four categories: those that review a lifetime of creative experience, such as Li Ji's My Writing Experience, Li Helin's My Literary Career of Teaching and Learning - Preface to Li Helin's Selected Literary Essays, etc.; those that recall specific works, such as Yang Yiyan's On the Writing of the Novel "Red Rocks," Zhi Xia's The Creation of the Railroad Guerrillas, and Liang Bin's Memoirs of Searching for the Drafts of 'Beacon Pictures', etc.; for those who recall a certain period of literary experience, such as Shen Congwen's From New Literature to Historical Literature, Shi Zhecun's "Two Years in Zhendan", and Feng Zhi's "Once Upon a Time in Kunming"; and for those who recall their literary interactions, such as Xu Qinwen's "Me in the Letters of Lu Xun", Tang Tao's "Me and Xiang Xian", and Zhao Jiabi's "A Few Things Reminded of by Mao Shun's Last Letter to Me".

2. Self-defense, prove innocence

In the history of modern and contemporary Chinese literature, some writers have been criticized to varying degrees and even deprived of their right to write for a long time because of historical reasons. They have been excluded from the ranks of writers. After the 1980s, with the transformation of the mainstay ideology, the historical problems of these writers were gradually solved. Before and after solving the historical problems, these writers often defended themselves by creating memoirs. One of the main purposes of Ding Ling's creation of The World of Demons was to justify her so-called "Nanking defection". Since "Ding Ling had always been secretive about her experiences in Nanjing and kept her mouth shut"[1], rumors about her "Nanjing Mutiny" had always plagued her, and became a pretext for her criticism in various political campaigns. In the 1980s, Ding Ling tried her best to "rectify this major historical wrongdoing", but she was "interfered with and obstructed", so "she was determined to write this memoir to tell people the true story of her life."[2] Ding Ling's purpose of proving her innocence through writing her memoirs is not only reflected in the motivation of writing, but also in the process of writing and the tone of the narrative. On August 1, 1984, the Organization Department of the CPC Central Committee, with the approval of the Secretariat of the CPC Central Committee, issued the "Document No. 9 of the Central Organizational Group - Circular on the Restoration of the Reputation of Comrade Ding Ling", which restored her reputation completely. After achieving the goal of self-explanation, Ding Ling stopped writing her unfinished book, The World of Demons, on August 23, 1984. In terms of narrative tone, the memoir is filled with grief of complaining and the urgency to prove her innocence. This can be seen very clearly in the table of contents of the memoir. The titles of sections 9 and 11 of the memoirs are respectively "Death is not easy" and "Is it a stain to deceive the enemy? "

(ii) Autobiographies organized by others

In the early 1980s, most of the old writers entered the twilight of their lives, old and frail, mobility is not easy, some writers write their memoirs in person has been more difficult, but they still feel that their own literary career or life history and modern China's historical changes have a close connection, or there are some about themselves, friends and relatives of the major events have to account for. Therefore, they decided to write their memoirs by dictating them to others, who then helped them organize and edit the material.

---

1 Li Xiangdong and Wang Zengru, Ding Ling's Biography, Zhongguo Daxue Quanshu Publishing House, 2015, p. 710.

2 Chen Ming, Title, The Elf World - The World of Snow and Wind, People's Literature Publishing House, 1989, p. 4.

So, they take the method of oral narration by themselves, and the assistance of others to organize and write memoirs. This kind of memoir is more representative of Xu Jie's "Footprint on the Bumpy Road". This memoir was serialized in the first issue of New Literary Historical Materials from 1983 to the end of the fourth issue in 1987, a total of 17 issues.[1] At the end of these 17 issues, there is a note saying that "Ke Ping assisted in organizing". In 1997, Footprint on the Bumpy Road was published by the East China Normal University Press, and the cover of the book showed the author contribution more clearly "Oral narration by Xu Jie and written by Ke Ping." Compared with the memoirs written independently by the writers themselves, the influence of this writing style on the narrative characteristics of the memoirs and even on the emotional color and ideology needs to be further studied.

Compared with this kind of writing style in which the writer himself narrates and others organize and write, Mao Dun's The Road I Walked and Hu Feng's Hu Feng's Memoirs are more worthy of attention. Mao Dun's memoirs, which had a great impact in the 1980s, were serialized in the first series of New Literary Histories from November 1978 until the end of 1986, when it was published in the fourth series.

Overall, it was published in 33 installments over 8 years. However, this long memoir was not entirely written by Mao Dun. The first issue of New Literary Historical Materials, published in 1983, was preceded by an editor's note: "The part of Comrade Mao Dun's memoirs that he wrote himself has already been published; the part that has continued to be published since the present issue was compiled by his relatives on the basis of audio recordings, conversations, notes, and other materials made by Comrade Mao Dun during his lifetime." In other words, in a strict sense, Mao Dun's memoirs were written only up to 1934, and although the 16 subsequent memoirs still use the

1 No. 3, 1985, and No. 1 and 2, 1986, were not serialized.

first-person pronoun "I" in the narrative, it is hard to say whether they still represent Mao Dun's attitude when he looked back at history in the 1980s.

The Memoirs of Hu Feng were written with the intention of testifying for himself. In the 1980s, Hu Feng had been waiting for his historical problems to be solved as soon as possible. In 1980, Hu Feng's historical problems were partially vindicated, but not completely solved. Therefore, until his death, Hu Feng was making various efforts for his complete vindication, writing memoirs was one of the important ways. At the beginning of his memoirs, Hu Feng stated bluntly: "With regard to the Left League, the information provided by all of us needs to be supplemented and corrected. I was a participant for a certain period of time, so I have to provide what I experienced."[1]. However, Hu Feng's memoirs contain only six parts, starting with "In Yidu - Memoirs of the War of Resistance Against Japan No.3" published in New Literary History, No.4, 1985, and followed by 17 memoirs compiled by the author's relatives based on his manuscripts, diaries, letters, and other materials."[2] When the single volume was published by the People's Literature Publishing House in 1993, the content written by Hu Feng remained unchanged, but the part completed by Mei Zhi was re-edited, with not only textual revisions, but also "a few additions and deletions of content".[3]

(iii) Recollections from an interview

Some writers did not have the desire to write memoirs at that time, or did not have the time to write full-length memoirs, but because of their important position in the history of modern Chinese literature, or because they were participants in an important literary event, some scholars have

1 Hu Feng, "Memories Before and After Joining the Left League (I)", New Literary History, No. 1, 1984.

2 Editor's note to Hu Feng's "In Yidu - Memories of the Resistance III", in New Literary and Historical Materials, 1985, no. 4.

3 Mei Zhi, "Afterword to the Preparation", in Hu Feng's Memoirs, Renmin Wenxue Publishing House, 1993, p. 427.

interviewed them according to the need for research, and these interviews have been published after being reviewed by the writers and have left precious historical materials for us. The most representative memoir of this kind is Zhou Yang's Laughing Talks about Historical Achievements. From the founding of the Leftist League to the early 1980s, Zhou Yang had been an important leader of left-wing literature in China, except for a few periods. But in the 1980s, when Hu Feng, Ding Ling, Xia Yan, Yang Han-sheng and Xu Maoyong published their memoirs, Zhou Yang's memoirs or recollections of Zhou Yang were rare. [1] This is a great pity for us to study Zhou Yang and the trend of modern Chinese literature. This is a great pity for our study of Zhou Yang and modern Chinese literary thought.

Under such conditions, the interview recorded by Zhao Haosheng, "Zhou Yang laughs about the merits and demerits of history" is also invaluable. In this memoir, Zhou Yang's courage to face historical achievements in the 1980s is admirable, and his gesture of "laughing about historical achievements and faults" is even more saddening.

(iv) Re-published autobiographical text

In addition to the re-published memoirs in the "Chinese Modern Writers on Creative Writing Series" published by Shanghai Literary and Art Publishing House, some of the more important memoirs include Shen Congwen's "Autobiography of Congwen", Hu Feng's "A book of three hundred thousand words", Ba Ren's "Handbook of Traveling to Guangzhuang" and "Autobiography"[2], and Xu Qinwen's "Autobiography of Qingwen", among others. Starting from 1948, when he was criticized in Hong Kong's Popular Literature and Art Series, Shen Congwen's situation in the mainland literary

1 Recollections of Zhou Yang, edited by Wang Meng and Yuan Ying, was published by the Inner Mongolia People's Publishing House in 1998; Xu Qingquan's Zhou Yang in the Eyes of the Informed was published by the Economic Daily Press in 2003.
2 According to Wang Keping, son of Ba Ren, the first draft of Journey to Guangzhi was completed in 1963, and the Autobiography is a material written by Ba Ren in 1950.

world became increasingly serious, and eventually disappeared. In the 1980s, when he reappeared, many people no longer knew Shen Congwen as a writer. Shen Congwen in his autobiography of the reissue of the "Note" said: "Nowadays, among intellectuals of forty or fifty years old who grew up in big cities, there are very few people who know what do I do; even for some of the professional peers, it is also very difficult to have the opportunity to read my past works."②[1]Under such circumstances, the republication of "Autobiography of Congwen" was of extraordinary significance for the dissemination of the writer's image.

The "A book of three hundred thousand words" had brought Hu Feng and his friends and relatives a catastrophe. It was used as important evidence to criticize him. In order to completely change Hu Feng's image from the depths of people's hearts and prove his innocence, we must let people see the original face of the "A book of three hundred thousand words". Thus, after the Office of the Central Committee of the Communist Party of China issued the "Supplementary Notice on Further Vindication of Hu Feng" on June 18, 1988, New Literary and Historical Materials, No. 4, 1988, reprinted the first, second and fourth parts of the "A book of three hundred thousand words" in nearly 120 pages. This long article, named "Report", is very much in the nature of a memoir, not to mention the first part which "describes the situation I experienced from around the time I entered the liberated areas in 1949 until the beginning of the examination"[2], is basically a memoir, and even the second part, "Explanatory Materials on a Few Theoretical Issues", is also a theoretical explanation and a refutation of the past on the basis of recollection. Therefore, in a certain sense, the "A book of three hundred thousand words"

1 Shen Congwen, Autobiography of Congwen (I) - Annotations, New Literary History, No. 3, 1980.
2 Hu Feng: Hu Feng 300,000 Words, Hubei People's Publishing House, 2003, p. 36.

is a memoir with strong theoretical summarization, and the reissue of this memoir is to a large extent to prove Hu Feng's innocence.

II. Writings on commemoration of writers

(i) Spontaneous reminiscences

In the 1980s, some writers passed away due to various reasons, and their friends and relatives either honored their historical contributions, grieved for what happened to them, or remembered their untimely deaths, or in order to redress their grievances, or in the hope of giving them a fair historical appraisal, they wrote memoirs under the inspiration of the Party Central Committee's historical reformation, trying to outline the image of the writers in their own minds. There are many such articles in the New Literary and Historical Materials, which can be broadly categorized according to their contents as follows:

The first category is to recognize historical contributions. This kind of reminiscence article is the most numerous, because when friends and relatives reminisce about the authors, a very important purpose is to commend their contributions to the history of modern Chinese literature. However, there are some special cases. Some of the reminiscence writings are added after the positive image of the writer has been established, such as Xu Qinwen's reminiscences of Lu Xun in his article "Brick Tower Hutong", "Lu Xun and Tao Yuanqing", "The Book of Blessings", and "Come to the Present Day". Some of them are comprehensive introductions, and some of them are not. There are some comprehensive introductions to writers who are often considered not comprehensive enough in previous literary history, such as Li Xiu's In Memory of My Father Li Guangtian, Xu Shihu's Li Jianwo's Life, Zhou Qisong's Memories of Xu Dishan, Bingxiong's Memories of Our Fathers: Qian Xuantong, and Memories of Our Father: Mr. Liu Bannong, by Liu Xiaohui and others. Mr. Liu Bannong" and so on. There is also another category that emphasizes the revolutionary contribution of writers, such as

Zhang Zhan's Xiao San and the National Salvation Times, Lou Shiyi's Remembering Xiao San, and Wu Liping's Comrade Pan Hanyuan, who waged a resolute struggle against the Kuomintang's cultural "encirclement and suppression".

The second category consists of writers seeking to reestablish their image. Some writers have been criticized for a long time due to historical reasons, and they have appeared before the world as the negative teaching material of the criticized writers in the history of literature. After the ideological transformation, the historical value of these writers has been reevaluated, and the status of some of them in literary history has been greatly enhanced. In order to reconstruct the literary history of these writers, in addition to the writers themselves writing memoirs to clear their names or republishing their memoirs, their relatives and friends also wrote memoirs that helped reestablish their literary history. For example, in the third issue of New Literary History in 1980, there were reminiscences in honor of Qu Qiubai: Qu Duyi's *In Memory of My Father*, Shi Lianxing's *Comrade Qiubai's Eternal Life*, Zhuang Dongxiao's *Comrade Qu Qiubai in the Central Soviet Area*, and the collection of reminiscences published by the People's Literature Publishing House in 1981, *Remembering Qu Qiubai*, etc. These memoirs not only reestablished the great image of Qu Qiubai as a revolutionary figure, but also affirmed his position in the history of literature as "one of the main founders of the proletarian revolutionary literary movement in China"[1].

The third category is of the nature of rediscovery. The difference between this category and the previous one lies in the fact that while the previous category of writers "existed" in the literary world or in academic research before the 1980s, only in a negative way, this category of writers had already

1 Zhou Yang, "Paving a Bright Path for Everyone" - Commemorating the 45th Anniversary of the Lifetime of Mr. Qu Qiubai", in Remembering Qiubai, People's Literature Publishing House, 1981, p. 6.

been "forgotten" in the literary world or in the literary-historical narrative before the 1980s, and their names were almost forgotten by the majority of the population. However, in the trend of rewriting literary history, their literary value has been reevaluated, and their names have gradually become known to readers through the memoirs of their friends and relatives. A prominent example is Zhu Xiang. There are ideological reasons for the "disappearance" of Zhu Xiang, but the more important reason is that he died young. In the 1980s, he was able to re-enter the public eye, and the changes in the times were naturally a crucial factor.

Moreover, the efforts made by Luo Niansheng and others in promoting the image of Zhu Xiang and evaluating her literary value should not be underestimated. Not only did Luo Zhansheng, together with Luo Xiaolan and Xu Xiacun, spread Zhu Xiang's image in articles in the New Literary Historical Materials[1], but he also spent a great deal of effort in promoting Zhu Xiang's reappraisal and publishing her posthumous works.

There are quite a number of writers who have been "forgotten" by history for ideological reasons, such as Zhang Henshui, Chen Mengjia, Xu Xu Xuan, Wang Wenxian, Lai Liewen and so on. When talking about the study of Zhang Henshui in the academic circles at that time, Zhang Youluan once said without regret: "Modern literary historians have all avoided talking about such an influential writer."[2]Therefore, in order to re-establish Zhang Henshui's place in modern Chinese literary history, not only is it necessary to re-publish his representative works, but it is also necessary to disseminate

1 Luo Niansheng, "Recollections of the Poet Zhu Xiang," Luo Yilan, "Books of Zhu Xiang," and Zhao Jingshen, "Biography of Zhu Xiang," New Literature Historical Materials, No. 3, 1982; Luo Niansheng, "Zhu Xiang's English Poems," New Literature Historical Materials, No. 1, 1984; and Xu Xiacun, "Zhu Xiang as I Knew Him," New Literature Historical Materials, No. 1, 1986.
2 Zhang Youluan, "Zhang Henshui, the Great Master of Episodic Novel," New Literary Historical Materials, No. 1, 1982.

the writer's image through articles of a reminiscent nature, and it is probably for such considerations that Zhang Youluan himself wrote reminiscences such as *Old Brother, Zhang Henshui* and *Zhang Henshui, the Great Master of Episodic Novels*.

The fourth category is remembrance of the deceased and narration of friendship. Of course, these articles also include accounts of the writers' contributions, but the main content is based on the writers' literary exchanges. The main memoirs of this kind published in New Literary Historical Materials include Gao Junzhen's *Lu Xun and Zheng Zhenduo*, Ge Baoquan's *Recollections of Days with Comrade Mao Dun* (6 articles), Fengzi's *Recollections of Comrade Ah Ying*, Qian Xiaohui's *The Friendship between My Father Ah Ying and Comrade Li Zhihua*

Bian Zhilin's "Talking about the Old into a Monologue: In Memory of Shi Tuo", He Xi's "Remembering the Abolition of the Name", and Cheng Junying's "Memories of Lujin", etc.

(ii) Organized Reminiscence Texts

For many famous writers in the history of modern Chinese literature, the 1980s was a very special era. During this decade, many of them were vindicated, and many of them left this world. In order to honor their contributions to modern Chinese literature, to celebrate their rehabilitation during their lifetime or after many years of death, or to pay tribute to those who had just passed away, New Literary History organized more than 30 releases of memoirs of commemorative writers in the 1980s. These memoirs can be divided into four categories, depending on their contents: memorials for the death of writers, celebrations for the rehabilitation of writers, commemorative writings marking the fifth and tenth anniversaries of writers, and other general remembrance articles.

According to the "Mourning" column in the first series of New Literary Histories from 1978 to the fourth issue of 1989, 53 writers died between 1977 and 1989, plus the 11 in the "Chronology of Contemporary Chinese Literature" listed at the back of Hong Zicheng's History of Contemporary Chinese Literature and Mudan, who died in 1977 and is not recorded in either of these texts, making a total of at least 65 writers who died during this period. In the 1980s, the New Literary Historical Materials devoted a column to nine writers and organized articles to pay tribute to them. There were some differences among them: the columns of Guo Moruo, Mao Shuang, Ding Ling, Cao Jinghua, Ye Shengtao, Shen Congwen, and Xiao Jun used the term "mourning" or "remembrance", while the columns of Nie Gannu and Hu Feng used the term "Research". The difference may lie in the fact that when Nie Gannu and Hu Feng died, their reputation had not yet been rehabilitated; while the previous writers were either comrades of the revolution, or had been completely rehabilitated.

In the 1980s, five writers were commemorated in articles organized by the New Literary Historical Materials for their rehabilitation: Lao She, Tian Han, Qu Qiubai, Hu Feng, and Pan Hannian. All of these writers' reputations were rehabilitated after their deaths. The memorial columns of Lao Xie and Tian Han were "In Memoriam" or "In Mourning", for they were not only revolutionary or progressive writers, but also persecuted to death by the Gang of Four. Qu Qiubai and Hu Feng's column was "Research", and Pan Hannian's memorial article was not even in a column, but in the "Writers' Works" column. Their problems were relatively more complicated, even more sensitive, and although their reputations were restored, it seems that their publicity was not as grand as that of Lao She and Tian Han, but relatively more low-key. The evaluation between them is not only analyzed by history, but also by reality.

It is a Chinese tradition to organize commemorations of historical figures on every fifth and tenth day of the year. In the 1980s, the New Literary Historical Materials organized a series of commemorative articles on many writers. These include "Special Series on the 100th Anniversary of the Birth of Lu Xun", "Special Series on the 40th Anniversary of the Martyrdom of Yu Dafu", "Special Series on the 10th Anniversary of the Death of Feng Xuefeng", and "Speacial Studies on the 25th anniversary of Zheng Zhenduo", "Studies on 80th anniversary of Feng Xuefeng", "Studies on 15th anniversary of Tian Han", "Studies on the 20th anniversary of Lao She, Studies on 85th anniversary of Wang Renshu (Ba Ren); 6 articles on the 50th anniversary of the death of Xu Zhimo, 5 articles on the 25th anniversary of the death of Yang Jiang, 3 articles on the 35th anniversary of the death of Geng Ji Zhi, 3 articles on the 5th anniversary of the death of He Qifang; the last category of commemorative essays was not assigned a column, but was placed in the "Writers' Works" column together with other reminiscence essays. The different treatments of the memorial articles show, to a certain extent, the value judgment of different writers by the academia in the 1980s.

In addition to the three types of organized memoirs mentioned above, the New Literary History also organized some general memoirs in the 1980s. The publication of these memoirs was not to commemorate a recently deceased writer, nor to restore a writer's reputation in the academic world, nor is there any indication that they were commemorative activities on every fifth and tenth anniversaries. There may be a chance to reminisce about a famous writer. Such organized reminiscences were published four times in the New Literary History in the 1980s, namely, five articles in "Yu Dafu Special Edition", two articles in "Guo Moruo Studies" (published in the 2nd issue of 1980 and the 4th issue of 1982), and five articles in "Chen Xianghe's Selected Works", which is probably a commemoration of Chen Xianghe.

(iii) Reminiscences written at the request of the author's friends and relatives

After the death of some writers, their relatives and friends, either because of the sadness of their afterlife, or because of the unforgettable memories of the writers, or because of the opportunity of the publication of the writers' anthologies, ask the writers' former friends to write reminiscences for them, which is a kind of nostalgia for the writers, and to a certain extent can also be interpreted as a kind of manifestation of the writers' status in literary history. In an article reminiscing about Li Jianwu, Shi Tuo explained the reason for his writing: "I have been friends with Li Jianwu for fifty years, and in the spring of last year, Comrade Wei Fan and Jengo's little daughter came to see me: Wei Fan worked in Beijing Modern Literature Museum and came to ask for the letter written by Jianwu to me; Jianwu's youngest daughter worked in Literature and Art Newspaper and hoped that I would write something in memory of her father."[1] Unable to refuse, Shi Tuo wrote "Remembering an old friend who was 'smooth in his dealings with others but principled at heart'" in memory of Mr. Li Jianwu with deep feelings. Another example is the article remembering the writer Li Yuran. After the death of Li Yuran in November 1984, his children wrote to Ding Ling, "After my father's death, we read all the newspapers, but there was no one to pay tribute to him, thinking that my father was lonely before his death, and that his death was a sad one. Ding Ling personally arrange "Chinese Literature," the second issue of 1985 to publish two poems by Li Yuran, the third issue published Liu Haihai's memorial article "Remembering Yuran".[2] It seems that there are more articles recalling writers when they are invited by their friends and

1 Shi Tuo: "Remembering an Old Friend of "Outside Roundness, Inside Squareness"", New Literary History, No. 2, 1987.
2 Li Xiangdong and Wang Zengru, Ding Ling's Biography, Zhongguo Da Baxue Quanshu Publishing House, 2015, p. 756.

relatives to write prefaces to their collections, such as "Recollecting a Talk between Xiao Hong and Me - Preface to Xiao Hong's Selected Works" (Nie Gannu), "Remembering the Evaluation of Plum - For the Publication of Shi Pingmei's Collected Works" (Lu Jingqing), and "The Endlessness of Zhi Di: The Selected Works of Song Zhidi" (Lu Jingqing), "A True Man - Preface to the Selected Novels and Prose of Chen Xianghe" (Chen Baichen), and so on.

(iv) Letters or Chronology with Memories Organized and Annotated by Friends and Relatives

In the 1980s, in the process of promoting the historization of modern literary research in China, the letters of many writers were compiled and published. These letters were private correspondence and they play an important role in furthering the study of the writer. Because of the distance of history and private nature, many contents of the letters are difficult to be understood by readers, therefore, some letters are published with a considerable amount of notes. These notes aim to explain the background of the writing of the letters, revise some of the contents of the letters, or even use some of the contents of the letters as an opportunity to develop richer memoir writing. Representative works of this kind of memoirs are *Xiao Jun's series of annotations*, *Selected Letters of Xiao Hong with Annotations*, and *Annotated Transcript of Letters from Lu Xun to Xiao Jun and Xiao Hong*. When introducing the original intention of annotating Xiao Hong's letters and briefs, Xiao Jun explained: "In August 1977, when I moved to live in Dongbahe Village in the eastern suburb of the capital, I picked up this batch of briefs from the pile of old papers."[1] "I decided to put this batch of briefs into a collection," he said, "and that it would be a good idea for me to make a copy of them with a brush and add appropriate annotations, thinking that they would be of some reference use to those who are interested in studying the life, thoughts,

1 Xiao Jun: Xiao Hong Shujian jianxue zhu xuezhi - Hou ji, Heilongjiang People's Publishing House, 1981, p. 4.

feelings, and life of this short-lived writer."[1] Xiao Jun seemed to have gathered a lot of courage when he decided to publish this collection. "Isn't a true materialist fearless? Therefore, I am going to publish all the briefs - including my own - here; and those that are to be 'annotated' will be honestly annotated. And those who want to 'borrow' anything from it can pick and choose whatever they want! Then just shoot it back!"[2] From these remarks of Xiao Jun, we can clearly feel the significance of this collection of writing and the historical value of Xiao Jun's annotations. Therefore, New Literary and Historical Materials, in 1979, Series 2-5, published 42 letters and briefs of Xiao Hong with Xiao Jun's annotations in four installments, and in the form of annexes, published four letters and briefs from Xiao Jun to Xiao Hong, as well as four other annexes and materials. In 1981, Heilongjiang People's Publishing House published a single-volume edition of Xiao Hong's Writing with Annotations.

III. Memories of Literary Societies, Literary Movements, Literary Newspapers and Publications, or Important Literary Historical Facts

(i) Spontaneous Recollections

1. Preservation of Literary Historical Materials

In the twilight of their lives, some writers who took part in the major literary events in the history of modern Chinese literature, in the spirit of being responsible for history and preserving historical materials for the future generations, spontaneously wrote a large number of memoirs recalling the literary societies, literary movements, literary newspapers or major literary historical facts. These essays provided valuable first-hand historical

1 Xiao Jun: Xiao Hong Shujian jianxue xiaohong shu jianxue zhu xuexue - Hou ji, Heilongjiang Renmin Publishing House, 1981, p. 4.

2 Xiao Jun: Xiao Hong Shujian jianxue xiaohong shujian zhu xuexue - Houjie, Heilongjiang People's Publishing House, 1981, p. 130.

information for the rewriting of literary history in the 1980s. In terms of content, these memoirs can be divided into the following categories:

Memoirs of Literary Societies. In the history of modern Chinese literature, a large number of influential literary societies have emerged, nurturing and uniting most modern writers. Preserving the historical materials of these literary societies is the historical basis for further writing and research on the history of modern Chinese literature. Memoirs published by Literary societies in New Literary History in the 1980s can be categorized into three main types: the Leftist League and its affiliates, the liberation area literary societies, and other progressive literary societies of the 1920s and 1930s. For example, Zhao Mingyi's *How the Left-Wing Dramatists' League was Formed*, *Recollections of the Left-Wing Dramatists' League*, Wang Yaping's and Liu Qian's *The Chinese Poetry Society*, Yang Jianru's *Miscellaneous Recollections of the Left-Wing Writers' League of the Northern China*, Liu Jinman's *Historical Recollections - Review of Several Poetry Organizations and Publications of the Liberation Areas*, Zhong Jingzhi's *Sidelight on the Overview of the Yan'an Lu Xun Academy of Arts*, and Chen Ming's *The First Year of the Northwest War Service Corps*, *Memories of the Taihang Literary Union* by Yutang, Some Information on the Cultivation of Young Writers by the Literary Union of the Jinsui Border Region by Ma Feng, *Lu Xun and the Creation Society* by Feng Naichao, *About the Establishment of the Literary Research Society* by Guo Shaoyu and *About the Sun Society* by Renjun, among others.

Literary Newspaper Memoirs. The New Literary History of the 1980s published a lot of memoirs of important literary newspapers and magazines of modern Chinese literature, but there are also many important literary newspapers and magazines that do not have any memoirs, such as of the Creation Society's Creation Quarterly, Creation Monthly, Creation Weekly, the Monthly of the Sun Society, and July and Hope of the July School. Memoirs published by New Literary and Historical Materials on modern literature include *Zheng Zhenduo and the Changes of the Novel Monthly* narrated by Gao Junzheng and written by Zheng Erkang, and *Miscellaneous Memories of the Modern Times (I, II, III)* by Shi Zhecun, *Miscellaneous Recollections of Chinese Poetry Forum* dictated by Huang Ningying during illness and recorded by Huang Li, Chen Canyun's *Ode to the Age of Storms and Clouds - Preface to Selected Poems of Chinese Poetry Forum*, Xiao Qian's *Fish Bait - Discussion Forum - Positions - Memories of the Grand Communal Newspaper Literature and Arts, 1935-1939*, Li Jianwu's *About Renaissance*, Hu Shanyuan's *I edited the 'Declaration of Free Talk*, Feng Zhi's Recollections of Sinking Bell- Preface to the Semi-Monthly Photocopied Edition of Sinking Bell, and so on.

Memoirs of literary works. These memoirs are mainly concerned with works that have had a significant impact on the history of modern literature or have a special significance for the writer. Unlike writers' articles about their own works, these memoirs are mainly about the works of others. Memoirs of literary works published in New Literary History in the 1980s include: Shen Weide's *Recollections of the First Performance of Metamorphosis, and on the Evaluation of Metamorphosis*, Xiao Qian's *Snow and the New Literary Movement in China: Remembering 'Living China'*, Zhu Zhengming's *On the Long March and the Words Given by Chairman Mao to Ding Ling*, *Forty-one Years of Talking about the Changing Times* by Mei Zhi recalling Hu Feng's preservation of Chairman Mao's words to Ding Ling, *A Chronicle of Mr. Lao Xie's Revision of the Drafts of 'The First Half of My Life* by Yu Haocheng, *The Issue of Shafei's Prototypes* by Xu Xiacun, and *Me and the Red Rocks* by Zhang Yu, and so on.

Memoirs of literary activities. Specifically, these memoirs are categorized into the following categories: editing and publishing, literary campaigns, literary events and literary performances. In the 1980s, Zhao Jiabi, a famous literary publisher, wrote a number of memoirs to reconstruct his efforts in publishing modern literature.

The New Literary History published seven of these articles, covering Lu Xun, China's New Literature, World Short Story Series, One Corner Series, and Collection of Soviet Writers. Later, a single volume, Editorial Memories of Lu Xun, Editorial Memories of the Past, and Literary Records of the Past: A Sequel to Editorial Memories of the Past, was published as a single volume. The memoirs of the literary movement are mainly about the liberated areas, such as Ding Ling's Before and After the Yan'an Literary Talks, Lei Jia's Literary and Artistic Activities in Yan'an in the Early 1940s (I-IV), Wang Yaping's Literary and Artistic Activities in the Hebei-Shandong-Henan Liberated Area, and so on. In the history of contemporary literature, the literary events that attract more attention are Hu Feng and Ding Ling. Because of the sensitivity of the events themselves, spontaneous memoirs of these events are not very common, and the only important ones in the New Literary History are Lin Mohan's oral account and Huang Huaying's The Before and After of Hu Feng's Incident: Lin Mohan's Questions and Answers, Book 1, and Li Zhilian's The Unwarranted Stories - Recollections of How the Ding Ling Issue Was Handled in 1955-1957. Literary performances were an important means for the Communist Party to carry out literary broadcast, and some memoirs of Communist-led literary performances in the history of modern literature also appeared in the New Literary History of the 1980s, such as Zheng Da's Drama Team's Overseas Broadcasts Kinds of Memories - Recollections of the Chinese Song and Dance Drama Society's Tours of the Southeast Asian Countries, and Battles inside and outside of the National Gate - Miscellaneous Recollections of the Activities of the Fifth Drama Team in Yunnan-Burma, Wu Qiang's Memories of the Cultural and Artistic Activities of the New Fourth Army, Ge Feng's Recollections of an Unusual Performing Activity of the Anti-Enemy Drama Society, and Yue Ye's The Long

Wind and the Waves are Still Dreaming of a Long Time - Recollections of Three Years' Performances in the South China Sea, and so on.

2. Proof of historical "truth"

Different writers will naturally have different memories of the same period of literary history due to differences in their positions, degrees of involvement, and memories. Thus, when the memoirs of a writer are published, other writers tend to revise, add or even refute them. For this reason, since the beginning of the third series, the new literary history has opened a "letter excerpts" column, specializing in the publication of the previous memoirs of the debates on the information or articles. Many of them are scholars' revisions of the facts of writers' memoirs based on research or evidence, and many of them are related to writers who questioned the facts based on their own memories, and there are even writers who seriously refute the contents involving themselves. For example, in order to clarify some of the questions surrounding the "two slogans" controversy in the 1930s, Mao Dun published *The Need to Clarify Some Facts in the second series of New Literary History* in 1979. In the 1950s, Li Rei, who was the leader of the literary and artistic circles in Henan Province, published *Statement on a Chapter of Yao Xueyin's "Fifty Years of Study and Pursuit* in order to refute the contents of Yao Xueyin's *Fifty Years of Study and Pursuit*. Later, Yao Xueyin published *Please Clarify the Historical Facts (Letters for Publication)*, which refuted Li's statement.

In the second half of 1986, due to the publication of two interviews on Zhou Zuoren's pseudo-post in the fourth issue of *Literary and Educational Materials*, *Reasons for Zhou Zuoren's Pseudo-Post* and *Summary of the Interview with Comrade Xu Baoren*, there was a strong interest in Zhou Zuoren's pseudo-post in the academic circles. However, the two interviewees soon published their retrospectives, unanimously denying the authenticity of the two interviews and showing the seriousness of their retrospectives with titles such as *Zhou Zuoren's Experience of Undertaking the Pseudo-post of Education Supervisor in North China* and *My Statement on Zhou Zuoren's Appointment to the Pseudo-post.* The fact that Zhou Zuoren had taken up a pseudo-post seemed to have been settled, but the skepticism continued unabated from the late 1980s into the 21st century.

(ii) Systematic reminiscences

To highlight the significance of certain major events in modern literary history, every five or ten years, some organizations and institutions organize commemorative articles to mark the occasion. In the 1980s, New Literary History organized and published two articles of this kind: the first was a series of 13 articles on the 60th anniversary of the May Fourth Movement, published in the third issue of 1979; the second was a series of 16 articles on the 50th anniversary of the founding of the Left League, published in issue No. 1 of 1980. The "Literary Memoirs of the Isolated Island of Shanghai" (Volume 1 and Volume 2), published by the China Social Science Publishing House in 1985, is also of this nature. In the "Afterword" to the first volume, the editors describe their method of work: "We have organized our efforts to compile this work after a relatively extensive survey. This collection is the first part of a literary memoir, primarily featuring contributions from senior writers, cultural figures, or family members and close friends of the writers in question." In organizing the publication of these essays, the organizers naturally saw the literary and historical significance behind them. "It has been forty to fifty years since the 'isolated island' period in Shanghai. The young people who were full of energy are now old men, and our work is therefore of a rescue nature, which makes us feel a heavy burden on our shoulders."[1] The great commemorative activities or compilations highlight on the one

1 ①Shanghai Academy of Social Sciences, Institute of Literature: "Memoirs of Shanghai's 'Isolated Island' Literature (Part I)· Afterword," China Social Sciences Press, 1984, pp. 439–440.

hand the special role of these events or organizations in the history of modern literature, and at the same time, provide the first-hand information for further academic research on these literary events or literary societies.

The above three classifications of writers' memoirs in the 1980s are based on more than 950 memoirs in the 45 issues of New Literary History from the first series of 1978 to the fourth issue of 1989, as well as on nearly a hundred works of writers' memoirs published in the 1980s. Although we cannot say that we have exhausted the types of memoirs of all writers in the 1980s, we should be able to show the overall picture of the memoirs of writers in the 1980s.

The Significance, Present Situation and Possibilities of Research on Memoirs of Writers in the 1980s

I. Reconstructing the Literary History of the 1980s: The Significance of the Study

In spite of disagreements and controversies, the "Historicization of Contemporary Literature", the "Re-entry into the Eighties", and the organization and study of historical materials of contemporary literature have been actively and steadily developed under the initiative and promotion of such famous writers as Hong Zi-cheng, Cheng Guang-wei, Wu Xiu-ming, Wu Jun, and so on, and have become a hot spot in the study of contemporary Chinese literature. It has become a hot spot in contemporary Chinese literary research. In the academic trend of "returning to the eighties", the writing of writers' memoirs should become a field that cannot be ignored. In terms of transcending the framework of academic cognition of the literature of the 1980s since the new era, it is of great significance: these writers' memoirs not only help us to re-examine some important issues in the history of modern Chinese literature, but also help us to re-conceptualize the ecological environment and developmental lineage of the literature of the 1980s, and help us to re-examine the imagination and construction of literary history of the 1980s in China. The writing of writers' memoirs was a prominent literary phenomenon in the 1980s. The New Literary History, founded in 1978, mainly focused on publishing "memoirs and biographies of Chinese writers since May Fourth"[1]. The "New Literary History Series" published by People's Literature Publishing House, the "Chinese Modern Writers on Creative Writing Series" published by Shanghai Literature and Arts Publishing House, the "Memories and Reflections" published by Hong Kong Sanlian Bookstore, and the "Camel Series" published by Hunan People's Publishing House. Memoirs of writers,

1 "To the Reader", New Literary History, No. 1, 1978.

such as Mao Dun, Ba Jin, Hu Feng, Ding Ling, Bing Xin, Xia Yan, Zang Kejia, Yang Han-shen, Xu Mao, Chen Baichan, Zhao Jiabi, Cao Jinghua, Xu Jie, Wang Xiyan, Yao Xueyin, Liang Bin, Chen Xuezhao, as well as reminiscences of writers such as Lu Xun, Guo Moruo, Mao Shuang, Lao She, Hu Feng, Ding Ling, Shen Congwen, Feng Xuefeng, Qu Qiubai, Yu Dafu, and Tian Han have appeared in large numbers. In the history of modern and contemporary Chinese literature, such a concentrated and large-scale publication of writers' memoirs is probably comparable only to the 1930s.

However, in the literary field of the 1980s, the old generation of writers who had worked hard in the history of modern literature since the May Fourth Movement and their numerous memoirs had been neglected. Ding Ling once complained that "some critical articles have paid more attention to the new writers than to the old ones".[1] One of the main reasons for her founding of China magazine was that she felt that "It is difficult for older writers to publish their works, and some publications do not treat new and established writers equally."[2] The literature of the eighties, under the spiritual banners of "New Enlightenment" and "Modernism", has severely shielded the memoirs of these old writers. This not only caused the neglect of writers' memoirs in literary criticism in the 1980s, but also still dominates our narrative of the literary history of the 1980s. In our literary history, there is almost no place for memoirs in the literature of the 1980s. If we are to effectively "return to the 1980s" with the academic concept of "historicizing contemporary literature," we should not remain silent on such concentrated and large-scale writing of authors' memoirs.

There are two main reasons why previous academic studies have neglected these huge numbers of writers' memoirs. One is that the "literary

---

1 Li Xiangdong and Wang Zengru, Ding Ling's Biography, Zhongguo Da Baike Quanshu Publishing House, 2015, p. 729.

2 Li Xiangdong and Wang Zengru: Ding Ling Biography, Zhongguo Da Baxue Quanshu Publishing House, 2015, p. 731.

character" of these memoirs is indeed not high, and the other is that our knowledge and understanding of the literary history of the 1980s are still restricted by the cognitive framework formed in the 1980s. In the 1980s, those who created memoirs were mainly "old writers" since the May Fourth Movement, and their main purpose of writing memoirs was not to pursue "pure literature", but to review, summarize, reflect on, and defend themselves. Their main purpose of writing memoirs is not to pursue "pure literature", but to review, summarize, reflect, complain, and even use it as a means to fight for their position in the literary world of the 1980s and in the history of modern Chinese literature. At that time, the reason why their memoirs did not cause too much reaction was closely related to the literary ecology of the 1980s. Literature in the 1980s was mainly aimed at "depoliticization" and "pure literature", and people were concerned with

"New Enlightenment" and "Modernism". In such a literary environment, memoirs of writers with little "literariness" value and often with certain ideological coloring naturally could hardly arouse the interest of the critics. But thirty years later, when we "return to the eighties", when we hope to "historicize" this period of literary past, the focus of our attention should not still be restricted by the cognitive framework of the eighties. Otherwise, such "historicization" is still a kind of imitation and repetition of the literary criticism of that year, and we can hardly see a complex, diversified and three-dimensional and full-bodied 1980s. While seeing the "Golden Age" of literature in the 1980s with "new writers", "New Enlightenment" and "Modernism", we should also have a better understanding of this Golden Age". At the same time, we should also conduct a historical review and summarize the efforts of these "old writers" who still have a strong influence in the literary world of the 1980s and their participation in the "reconstruction" of literary history mainly through the writing of memoirs.

Examining the presence of "old writers" in the literary field of the 1980s from the perspective of memoir writing is a novel and important way to help us examine the ideology, literary practice and the literary ecology formed by these writers in the 1980s. In the 1980s, the writing of writers' memoirs was an important way for many old writers to return to the literary world, and it should be an indispensable page in the literary history of the 1980s. These memoirs provide us with the "other half" of the 1980s literature, which has been seriously neglected by previous studies: a different literary landscape, literary trends, literary ecology and writers' spiritual personalities of the 1980s. They not only have an indispensable historical position in the non-fiction writing of the 1980s, but also provide us with a possibility to form overall outlines of the spirit of these writers in the twilight of their lives. It provides a possibility for the state of the art. At a time when the construction of contemporary literary history is being increasingly emphasized, the arrangement of historical materials, documentary analysis and comprehensive study of the memoirs of writers in the 1980s can not only provide us with a new perspective of "returning to the 1980s", but also provide historical support for the study of modern and contemporary literature in the future.

II. the seriously neglected literary historical facts: the current situation of the research

Although scholars such as Mr. Yang Zhengrun, Mr. Guo Jiulin, Mr. Zhu Wenhua, Mr. Gu Yeping and their doctoral students Zhu Xuchen, Guo Xiaoying, Lei Ying, Han Bin, and other scholars in the field of modern Chinese biography have also dealt with the memoirs of the writers of the 1980s to different degrees, due to the difference in their awareness of the problem, they have paid more attention to the theoretical construction of the modern Chinese biography, the outline of the history of literature, the analysis of the literary style and the aesthetic interpretation, and there has been little discussion on the position of writers' memoirs in the literary field of the 1980s and its role in the history of literature. However, due to the difference in problematic consciousness, they focus more on the theoretical construction of modern Chinese biography literature, literary history, genre analysis and aesthetic interpretation, but little has been said about the position of writers' memoirs in the literary field of the 1980s and their literary history.

In previous studies, memoirs of writers in the 1980s are mainly cited as historical materials. The only studies that have really taken them as objects of research are case studies, which mainly include the following aspects:

Study of *Lu Xun's Memoirs*. After the founding of New China, there have been many works on *Lu Xun's memoirs*, including Xu Guangping's *Memoirs of Lu Xun* published by the Writers' Publishing House in 1961, Shanghai Literature and Arts Publishing House's *Memoirs of Lu Xun (first collection)* published in 1978, and *Lu Xun's Memoirs (second collection)* published in 1979.

The six-book Recollections of Lu Xun, published by Beijing Publishing House in 1999, and *Xu Guangping's Recollections of Lu Xun (in manuscript)*, published by Changjiang Literature and Art Publishing House in 2010. Among them, the six volumes of Recollections of Lu Xun are divided into two parts: monographs and essays, each in three volumes, with a total of 2.4 million words. According to Zhu Zheng, an expert on Lu Xun Studies, this volume of memoirs is "quite complete", with "most of the important reminiscences published in the past few decades collected, with not much left out".[1] In this respect, Lu Xun's memoirs should be fairly well organized by now. However, there is not much research on Lu Xun's memoirs. So far, there is only one book, Zhu Zheng's The Corrections and Errors of Lu Xun's Memoirs, with more than 20 articles. The concerns include the authenticity

1 Zhu Zheng, "Why the Third Edition of Lu Xun's Memoirs was Printed", Lu Xun Research Monthly, No. 2, 2000.

of the contents of the various editions of *Lu Xun's Recollections* by Xu Guangping and others, the construction of Lu Xun's image, and the comparison between the manuscript version and the revised version of the Recollections.

Study of *Ba Jin's Memoirs*. Among the memoirs of writers in the 1980s, the one that has attracted the most attention is probably Ba Jin's Essays. So far, more than 120 papers have been published on this memoir, and six monographs and collections of essays have been published. The reason why Ba Jin's Essays has received so much attention may be related to Ba Jin's influence in the literary world in the 1980s, and on the other hand, it may also be due to the fact that Essays contains not only memoirs, but also many other contents, which leaves a relatively large space for further research. These research results are mainly related to: Ba Jin's sense of repentance, his thoughts in his later years, Ba Jin's personality and image construction, the issue of editions of Ba Jin's Memoir. , "Memoirs" as testimonial literature, "Memoirs" as prose, and so on.

The Autobiography of Shen Congwen was first published in 1934, so it is not within the scope of our study. However, for historical reasons, Shen Congwen disappeared from the Chinese literary scene in the 1950s, and by the time he came back in the 1980s, many people did not know this writer. This is just like what he said when he re-released his autobiography: "Nowadays, very few intellectuals in their forties and fifties who grew up in big cities understand what do I do; even some of my professional colleagues hardly have a chance to read my past works."[1] In this regard, the re-release of Autobiography of Congwen signified the rebirth of a writer. Since the 1980s, the research on Autobiography of Congwen has not been interrupted,

1 Shen Congwen, "Autobiography of Congwen (I) - Annotations", New Literary History, No. 3, 1980.

and more than 30 papers have been published, mainly focusing on the significance of Autobiography of Congwen for the study of Shen Congwen, the issue of its edition, its value as a biographical literature, and its comparison with biographies such as The Morning Flower and the Evening Gleanings and The Age of Youth, etc.

There are more than 40 research papers on Yang Jiang's Six Memoirs of a Cadre of Schools, one third of which are studies on it as testimonial literature, and one third of which are studies on it as a prose text. Other writers' memoirs that have been the subject of relatively more research include Ding Ling's The World of Demons and The World of Wind and Snow (7 essays, mainly on Ding Ling's characterization), Mao Dun's The Road I Walked (5 essays, mainly on Shen Weiwei's "corrections"), "Leisurely Pursuing Memories of Days Gone By" by Xia Yan (5 essays, mainly on its understanding as testimonial literature), and "The Broken Recollections of Cloudy Dreams" by Chen Baichen (5 essays, focusing on its value as testimonial literature).

There is only one article that studies the memoirs of writers in the 1980s as a literary phenomenon: "A Preliminary Discussion on the Memoirs of Old Writers in the 1980s: Taking New Literary Historical Materials as an Example" by Jin Xin. The article summarizes the intention of writing memoirs of writers in the 1980s, their contractual nature, sense of superiority, authenticity and sense of repentance. It is an important article for the study of writers' memoirs in the 1980s. However, as the title of the article suggests, it is only a "preliminary study", and many issues have not been explored in depth. Meanwhile, in terms of the production mechanism and production process of authors' memoirs in the literary field of the 1980s, the relationship between authors' memoirs and the literary field of the 1980s, the literary ecology reflected in the writing of authors' memoirs, and the ideological consciousness of a generation of intellectuals in the 1980s, there are many important issues that need to be studied more deeply and more extensively in this field.

From the above overview, it can be seen that compared with the memoirs of writers that appeared on a large scale in the 1980s, the number of studies on them is pitifully small. There is only one comprehensive research paper, and the rest of the less than 200 research papers and less than 10 research books are mainly about Lu Xun, Ba Jin, Shen Congwen, Yang Jiang, Ding Ling and so on. The present situation of such research is obviously incompatible with the concentrated and large-scale appearance in the memoirs of writers in the 1980s of the twentieth century.

The main reason for this is that we have not been examining them as a literary phenomenon, but only as documentary information to be examined and utilized. If we put them into the literary field of the 1980s for an overall study, it will not only open up the inner space of these writers' memoirs, but also promote the historicization process of the literature of the 1980s to a certain extent.

This work should still focus on a close reading of the text, with reference to other relevant historical sources, but it is very different from the use of these authors' memoirs in the past. In the past, academic research seldom used these memoirs as the object of study, but more often cited them as arguments in the study of a specific author or literary event. Our study, however, has a different quest. We wanted to analyze the memoirs of the writers of the 1980s as a complete literary object, rather than searching for evidence in the form of excerpts. We want to interpret the memoirs of writers as a complete text, without limiting ourselves to explaining their literary character. Our research is an external study based on close reading of texts and historical evidence, but leading to literary ecology and literary environment. It will go beyond the previous idea of using memoirs as arguments, and will not be confined to the "purely literary" approach of interpreting their literary nature through close reading of texts. Writers' memoirs are not only arguments for literary research, they can also be independent research objects; literary history research is not only the literary analysis of literary works, but it should also include the restoration and construction of the literary field and ecology. We hope to take the memoir writing of writers in the 1980s of the twentieth century as a present literary phenomenon, and take the text of memoir as the starting point of independent analysis. Our research wants to take into account the ups and downs of the writers in the history of Chinese modern and contemporary literature and their situation in the literary world of the new period, and presents a three-dimensional, rich and complex history of literature in the 1980s through the examination of this literary phenomenon.

III. Definition of concepts - Organization of historical materials - Textual analysis – Historical Construction: the rationale of the research

If we are to carry out the research on the memoirs of writers in the 1980s, we think that the following aspects may become the focus of attention.

1 . Definition and Scope of Memoirs of Writers in the 1980s

As far as the definition is concerned, there are two main questions to be solved: what is the relationship between memoirs and autobiographies of writers in the context of contemporary Chinese literature, and whether and how the details of memoirs can be fictionalized according to the requirements of literary creation.

So far, there is no basic organization of writers' memoirs in the 1980s, and they are scattered in various newspapers and magazines, writers' collections, prefaces and trilogies of monographs, and notes of letters. In terms of its style, it can be historical materials, essays, or even notes. In terms of its scope, the memoirs of writers in the 1980s can be roughly summarized as follows: (i) Autobiographical memoirs. This kind of situation accounts for most of the memoirs of writers in the 1980s, such as the "New Literary

History Series" published by the People's Literature Publishing House, and the "Modern Chinese Writers on Creative Writing Series" published by the Shanghai Literature and Art Publishing House, and so on. (ii) Biographical Memoirs. It is a reminiscence of the writer's words.

Compraring with autobiographical memoirs, these memoirs are generally shorter in length. For example, the People's Literature Publishing House published a collection of commemorative essays called *Remembering Qiubai* in 1981, and the Special Edition to Commemorate the 100th Anniversary of Lu Xun's Birth, Special Edition to Commemorate the 40th Anniversary of Yu Dafu's Martyrdom, and so on, published by the New Literary History Special Series in Commemoration of the 10th Anniversary of Feng Xuefeng's Death, and so on. (iii)Recollections of literary societies, literary movements, literary newspapers, or major literary historical facts. For example, the *Memories of the Left League (Volume I and Volume II)* published by the China Social Science Publishing House in 1982, *the Memorials to the 60th Anniversary of the May Fourth Movement* published by the New Literary History, a series of 13 articles, and a series of articles commemorating the 50th Anniversary of the founding of the Left League (16 articles), *Literary Recollections of the Orphaned Islands in Shanghai (Volume I and Volume II)* published by China Social Science Publishing House in 1985, and so on.

There are two genres that we do not think should be included in the memoirs of writers of the 1980s. One is the diary and the other is the biography. The main reason for not including diaries in the scope of writers' memoirs is that they lack the long, reflective perspective and vision of a memoir. General biographies, of course, cannot be included in memoirs, and even biographies with reminiscences written by the writer's friends and relatives are not suitable to be included in memoirs, in our opinion. Because there is a great difference in the nature of biography and memoir. Biography is based on historical information; it is a literary writing based on historical research. Memoir is based on memories; it is a historical construction based on subjective confidence in memories.

2. A review and summary of the life experiences and creative careers of "progressive" writers.

As far as autobiographical memoirs are concerned, memoirs that give an account of writers' life experiences and recall their creative journeys make up the majority.

Mao Dun's The Road I Walked, Ding Ling's The Wind and the Snow, Xia Yan's The Book of Old Dreams, Zang Kejia's Poetry and Life, and Yang Hansheng's Poetry and Life. Yao Xueyin's Fifty Years of Learning and Pursuing, Yang Jiang's Six Recollections of the Cadre School, and Chen Baichen's Broken Recollections of the Cloudy Dreams all belong to this category. If we put these memoirs in the literary field of the 1980s, the question we need to consider is: if they are understood as a kind of witness literature, what did the writers emphasize when they recalled their own life experience and creative process? What does the author emphasize and what does he avoid? What are his initial reasons for emphasizing and avoiding? What is the relationship between this and the literary environment of the 1980s? For example, in Mao Dun's The Road I Walked, the author claimed that "what I wrote down was always true. Words may be used in reply, or occasionally embellished, but the truth is not lost because of splendor"[1]. However, according to Prof. Shen Weiwei, there are no fewer than a hundred errors in the three volumes of Mao Shuang's memoirs, which are due to errors of memory as well as deliberate avoidance and concealment. [2] Why would a memoir

1 Mao Dun: The Road I Walked - Preface, The Road I Walked (above), People's Literature Publishing House, 1981, p. 1.
2 Shen Weiwei, "A Brief Comment on the Errors in Mao Dun's 'The Road I Have Traveled', Zhejiang Journal, 1990, No. 5

written under the standard of "truthfulness" have such deliberate evasions and cover-ups? If we consider the literary environment of the early 1980s, how should we interpret these "evasions and cover-ups"?

Not only autobiographical memoirs, but also the memories of writers by others, make up a large proportion of writers' memoirs in the 1980s, which review and summarize writers' life experiences and creative careers. The memories of friends and relatives, the remembrances of writers all aim to recognize their contributions to the history of modern Chinese literature. Some of these cases are worth paying attention to. Some memoirs are partially revised after the positive image of the writer has been established, for example, Lu Xun, from the deification, fragmentation and even distortion during the special period to the "human Lu Xun" in the New Enlightenment in the 1980s, the image of Lu Xun has changed a lot. In what ways are these changes reflected? How did the publication of Lu Xun's memoirs influence the reconstruction of Lu Xun's image in the 1980s? What are the characteristics and limitations of Lu Xun's memoirs in the 1980s compared with those of later historical materials? What are the implications for the study and dissemination of Lu Xun's image? Some of the memoirs are of a comprehensive nature, and such writers are often regarded as not having written comprehensively enough in the past literary history, for example, Li Guangtian, Li Jianwu, Xu Dishan, Shen Yinmo, Qian Xuantong, Liu Bannong, and so on. So, whataspects of these writers were emphasized and highlighted in the previous literary history? What about them remains unseen? What has been "restored" in the writers' memories of the 1980s? What are the reasons for this? On the other hand, there is more emphasis on the revolutionary contribution of writers, as in the memoirs of Xiao San, Pan Hannian, Feng Naichao, Hu Yuzhi and others. To emphasize the contribution of writers to the revolution, what kind of literary ecology did it reflect in the early 1980s?

Such reviews and summaries were sometimes published in the memoirs of writers in the 1980s in the form of commemorative albums organized in a series of articles. For example, in the 1980s, New Literary History opened a column to organize articles to pay tribute to nine writers who had just passed away, and to commemorate the birthdays or death anniversaries of 12 writers on every fifth and tenth day of their lives. However, there are differences between them. The terms used in the memorial columns for Guo Moruo, Mao Dun, Ding Ling, Cao Jinghua,

Ye Shengtao, Shen Congwen, and Xiao Jun were "mourning" or "remembrance," while the terms used in the memorial columns for Nie Gannu and Hu Feng were "research." The memorial columns of Lu Xun, Yu Dafu, and Feng Xuefeng are "annual specials", those of Zheng Zhenduo, Tian Han, Lao She, and Wang Renshu are "studies", and those of Xu Zhimo, Yang Gang, Geng Jizhi, and He Qifang do not even have columns. Instead, they were placed in the "Writers' Works" section together with other reminiscences. The different ways of handling writers' commemorative articles show, to a certain extent, the literary ecology of the 1980s and the value judgment in academia on different writers.

3. Proof of the innocence of "problematic" writers and the return of their literary status

In the history of modern and contemporary Chinese literature, some writers have been considered "problematic" for historical reasons, and have been subjected to different degrees of criticism, or even deprived of the right to literary creation for a long time, and excluded from the ranks of writers. In the 1980s, with the transformation of ideology, the historical problems of these writers were gradually resolved. In this process, writers' memoirs played an indispensable role, not only providing historical support for the writing of literary history, but also providing a sentimental basis for the dissemination of positive images of writers.

Some writers have defended themselves mainly by writing memoirs. One of Ding Ling's main goals in creating The World of Demons was to clear her name of the slanders that had been poured over her. Rumors of the "Nanking defection" continued to haunt Ding Ling, and became a source of criticism for her in successive political campaigns. In 1933, someone intentionally spread the rumor that Ding Ling had surrendered herself in Nanking; in 1955, someone used this as a weapon to criticized the "Ding and Chen Anti-Party Group"; this matter was raised again in 1957 during the "Anti-Rightist" campaign, and Ding Ling was expelled from the Party and dismissed from her post; later Ding Ling was imprisoned for being a traitor. In the 1980s, Ding Ling tried her best to "correct this major historical mistake", but was "disturbed and obstructed", so "she decided to write this memoir to tell the people about the real situation of that year. Therefore, "she decided to write this memoir to tell the people what really happened in those years".[1] Hu Feng's memoirs were also written with the intention of testifying for herself. Hu Feng always expected his historical problems to be solved as soon as possible. In 1980, Hu Feng's historical problems were partially solved, but not completely solved. Therefore, until his death, Hu Feng was making various efforts for his complete rehabilitation, and writing his memoirs was one of the important ways. At the beginning of this memoir, Hu Feng stated very frankly: "Concerning the Left League, the information provided by all of us needs to be supplemented and mutually corrected. I was a participant for a certain period of time, and I have to give an account of what I have experienced."[2]

---

1 Chen Ming, Title, The Elfin World - The World of Wind and Snow, People's Literature Publishing House, 1989, p. 4.

2 Hu Feng, "Memories of Joining the Leftist League Before and After (I)," New Literary History, No. 1, 1984.

Some writers choose to reissue memoirs that have been published before. For example, from 1948, when Shen Congwen was criticized in Hong Kong's Popular Literature and Arts Series, his situation in the mainland literary world became increasingly serious, and he eventually disappeared. In the 1980s, he came back and republished "Autobiography of Shen Congwen". The most important purpose is to re-establish his own image in literary history.

The republication of Hu Feng's "A Book of Three Hundred Thousand Words" in the 1980s can also be categorized as such. The "A Book of Three Hundred Thousand Words" once brought Hu Feng and his friends and relatives a catastrophe, and has been used as important evidence to criticize them. In order to change the image of Hu Feng from the depth of people's heart and prove his innocence, we must let people see the true nature of "A Book of Three Hundred Thousand Words". Therefore, after the General Office of the CPC Central Committee issued the "Supplementary Notice on Further rehabilitation of Hu Feng" on June 18, 1988, the "New Literary History" Issue No. 4 of 1988 re-released the "A Book of Three Hundred Thousand Words" with nearly 120 pages of the first, second and fourth parts. In a certain sense, "A Book of Three Hundred Thousand Words" is a memoir with a strong theoretical summary, and the re-publication of this memoir is to a large extent to prove Hu Feng's innocence.

In addition to the writers themselves writing memoirs or re-publishing the writers' previous memoirs, some individuals or organizations, in order to prove the writers' innocence and to re-establish the writers' historical image. For example, *the memoirs of Qu Qiubai* was published in the 3rd issue of New Literary History in 1980, and the collection of memoirs *Remembering Qu Qiuba*i was published by People's Literature Publishing House in 1981. Among these memoirs, there are Qu Duyi's Nostalgia for My Father, Zhou Yang's Paving a Bright Path for All - Commemorating the Forty-fifth Anniversary of Comrade Qu Qiubai's Righteousness, Mao Dun's Memories of the

Martyr Qubai, Ding Ling's Memories and Reflections on Comrade Qu Qiubai as I Knew Him, "Memories of Mr. Qu Qiubai" by Ye Shengtao, and so on. These articles not only re-established the great image of Qu Qiubai as a revolutionary, but also affirmed his literary historical status as "one of the main founders of the proletarian revolutionary literary movement in our country." [1]

Unlike the official organization of Qu Qiubai's memoirs, the memoirs of the "Hu Feng Anti-Revolutionary Group" case were mainly organized by Hu Feng's daughter Xiaofeng, and their publication was full of twists and turns. According to Xiaofeng herself, at the end of the 1980s, she "gathered together those who were implicated in the 'Hu Feng Anti-Revolutionary Group' case to write an article recalling the origins of their relationship with Hu Feng, the influence they had received, and what happened to them after they were branded as 'Hu Fengists'". After they had been branded as 'Hu Fengists', the collected articles were "compiled into a collection of many people, so as to leave some first-hand information for future generations". This was another effort of Hu Feng's family to reconstruct the image of Hu Feng and the writers affected by him in literary history after the "Hu Feng Counter-Revolutionary Group" was completely rehabilitated. However, due to the complexity of the 1980s, this endeavor sometimes became very difficult. The publication of this "multi-authored collection" was not a smooth process. "Due to the change of the objective situation, the publisher, who had been very enthusiastic, suddenly stopped mentioning it. The matter had to be put aside for three or four years."[2]In the end, this collection of memoirs,

1 Zhou Yang, "Paving a Bright Path for Everyone" - Commemorating the Forty-fifth Anniversary of the Righteousness of Qu Qiubai, in Remembering Qiubai, People's Literature Publishing House, 1981, p. 6.
2 Xiaofeng, "Hu Feng and I - Afterward", Ningxia People's Publishing House, 1993, p. 848.

which had been compiled in the late 1980s, was not published until 1993 by the Ningxia People's Publishing House.

The publication of some writers' memoirs is somewhat similar to the rediscovery of "lost" writers. The difference between this category of writers and the previous one lies in the fact that the writers of the previous category were "present" in the literary world or academic research prior to the 1980s, albeit in a negative light.

In contrast, the writers of this category were virtually forgotten in the literary world or literary history prior to the 1980s, and their names have been largely forgotten by most people. However, in the trend of rewriting literary history, their historical value has been reassessed and their names have been gradually made known to readers through the memoirs of their friends and relatives. Among them, there are Zhu Xiang, Liang Yu Chun, Mu Shi Ying, Wang Yiren, Wang Sidian who died young; there are also Shen Congwen, Zhang Henshui, Chen Mengjia, Xu Xu, Wang Wenxian, Li Liewen and so on who were "forgotten" by history because of ideological reasons. There are some ideological reasons for the "disappearance" of Zhu Xiang, but the more important reason is that he died young, and he was able to re-enter the readers' vision in the 1980s, the change of the time and environment is naturally the most important factor, and the efforts of Luo Niansheng and others in the propagation of the image of Zhu Xiang, and the evaluation of his literary value are also indispensable. The efforts of Luo Niansheng and others in publicizing Zhu Xiang's image and evaluating her literary value should not be underestimated. Luo Niansheng not only published articles in the New Literary History with Luo Xinlan and Xu Xiacun to disseminate the image of Zhu Xiang, but also spent a lot of effort in promoting the reevaluation of Zhu Xiang and the publication of Zhu Xiang's posthumous works.

4. The Missing Memoirs and the Literary Field of the 1980s

During the boom in autobiographical writing by writers in the 1980s, the number of memoirs by some writers who are extremely important in the history of modern Chinese literature, such as Zhou Yang, Cao Yu, Zhang Ailing, and Mu Dan, was extremely scarce. This is a phenomenon worth noting. From the founding of the Leftist League to the pre-1980s, Zhou Yang had been an important leader of left-wing literature in China, except for some periods. While Hu Feng, Ding Ling, Xia Yan, Yang Han-shen and others published their memoirs, the "absence" of Zhou Yang's memoirs and the "difficult birth" of The Collected Works of Zhou Yang could not help but strike a deep chord. Starting from this phenomenon, we may be able to touch upon the key connotations in the field of literature in the 1980s. From Wang Yao's Historical Draft of New Chinese Literature to the literary history of the 1980s, Cao Yu has always been an important presence. However, in the 1980s, there were not many memoirs of Cao Yu, and there was not even a single memoir of Cao Yu in the New Literary History, the most important periodical for the publication of writers' memoirs. This phenomenon is quite intriguing. For historical reasons, Zhang Ailing and Mudan were almost "absent" from literary history before the 1980s, but with the change of ideology, they became very popular again after the 1990s. In terms of their literary status, the 1980s was a very important turning point. However, compared with Zhou Zuoren who had been "betrayed his original political position and join the opposite enemy", the number of memoirs of these two writers in the 1980s is still too few, and the implication of this is worth exploring.

5. The Preservation of Literary Historical Sources and the Discernment of Literary Historical Facts

As far as the memoirs of the writers of the 1980s are concerned, in addition to further establishing or partially revising the literary status of the "progressive" writers, rehabilitating some of the "problematic" writers, and creating a new image in literary history, a large part of the memoirs concerns literary associations, literary newspapers and literary movements. The primary purpose of these memoirs is to provide historical material for the re-writing of literary history in the new era, and to correct the "distorted" literary historical material that has been previously published.

Memoirs of writers that have been preserved include: memoirs of literary societies, memoirs of literary newspapers, memoirs of literary works, and memoirs of literary activities. The literary society memoirs published in the 1980s mainly concerned the Leftist Writers' League and its subordinate organizations, literary societies in the liberated areas, and other progressive literary societies of the 1920s and 1930s. For example, Zhao Mingyi's "How the League of Left-Wing Dramatists was Formed" and "Memories of the League of Left-Wing Dramatists", Yang Qianru's "Miscellaneous Recollections of the League of Left-Wing Writers of the North", Wang Zhizhi's "Recollections of the League of Left-Wing Writers of the North", Zhong Jingzhi's "A Sidelight on the Yan'an Lu Xun Art Institute", Chen Ming's "First Year's Chronicle of Northwestern Field Service Corps", Ma Feng's "Training of Literary League of the Jingsui Youth District", Feng Naichao's "Lu Xun and the Creation Society", Guo Shaoyu's "On the Establishment of the Literary Research Society", and Ren Jun's "On the Sun Society", and so on.

In the 1980s, many memoirs of important literary newspapers and magazines on modern Chinese literature were published, but there were also very few memoirs of many important literary newspapers and magazines, such as Creation Quarterly, Creation Monthly, Creation Weekly of the Creation Society, Tai Yang Monthly of the Tai Yang Society, July and Hope of the July School and other progressive literary newspapers such as The Analects of Confucius, Yu Si and New Moon, and other progressive literary and artistic newspapers. Memoirs of literary works are mainly concerned with works that have had an important impact on the history of modern literature or have a special significance for the writers. The most representative memoirs of this kind are "Series on the Creative Writing of Modern Chinese Writers". Naturally, many of the memoirs collected in this series were not written in the 1980s, but a considerable proportion of them were written in the 1980s. Moreover, from the point of view of rewriting literary history, even the memoirs written before that time actually participated in the academic trend of reconstructing the history of literature in the 1980s.

If divided into specific categories, the memories of literary activities include the following: editing and publishing, literary campaigns, literary events and literary performances.

In the 1980s, Zhao Jiabi, a famous literary publisher, wrote a number of memoirs to reconstruct his efforts to publish modern literature. The memoirs of the literary movement are mainly about the liberated areas, such as Ding Ling's Before and After Yan'an Literary and Artistic Symposium, Lei Jia's Literary and Artistic Activities in Yan'an in the Early Forties (I-IV), and Wang Yaping's Literary and Artistic Activities in Jiluyu Liberated Areas. Among the literary memoirs of the 1980s, the more noteworthy literary events are mainly those of Hu Feng and Ding Ling. Because of the sensitivity of the events themselves, there are not many spontaneous memoirs about these events. Some of the more important ones include Lin Mohan's "Before and After the Hu Feng Incident: Interview with Lin Mohan (Part 1)", which was narrated by Lin Mohan and edited by Huang Huaying, and Li Zhilian's "Unwarranted Stories - Recollections of the Handling of Ding Ling's Problems in 1955-1957". Literary performances were an important means for the Communist Party to carry out literary and cultural publicity, and some memoirs of Communist-led literary performances in modern literary history were also published in the 1980s, such as Zheng Da's The Story of the Performing Drama Team Sowing Seeds Overseas - Recollections of the Chinese Song and Dance Drama Society's Tours of Nanyang, The Battles at the Gates of the Nation - Recollections of the Performing Drama Team's Activities in

Burma, Wu Qiang's "Recollections of the Literary and Artistic Activities of the New Fourth Army", Ge Feng's "Remembering an Unusual Performance by the Anti-Enemy Drama Club", and Yue Ye's "The Long Wind Breaks the Waves and the Dream is Still Warm - Remembering Three Years of Performances in Southeast Asia".

For the same period of literary history, different writers will naturally have different recollections because of their different positions, different degrees of participation and different contents of their memories. Therefore, when a writer's memoirs are published, other writers tend to revise, supplement and even refute them. For this reason, since the third series, the New Literary History has created a column called "Letter Excerpts", which is dedicated to the publication of information or articles debating the memoirs of previous issues. Many of them are scholars revising some facts of writers' memoirs according to research or evidence, and many of them are related writers questioning the facts according to their own memories, and some of them seriously refute the contents involving themselves. For example, in order to clarify some of the circumstances surrounding the "two slogans" controversy in the 1930s, Mao Dun published *The Need to Clarify Some Facts* in the second series of New Literary Historical Materials in 1979. In order to refute some contents of Yao Xueyin's *Fifty Years of Study and Pursuit*, Li Rui, who was the leader of the literary circles in Henan Province in the1950s, published *Statement on a Chapter of Yao Xueyin's Fifty Years of Study and Pursuit*, and later Yao Xueyin published *Please Clarify the Historical Facts (Letters)*, which refuted the statement of Li Rui.

6. The Production Mechanism of Writers' Memoirs in the 1980s

After sorting out and summarizing a large number of memoirs by writers of the 1980s, we need to explore and analyze the production mechanism of memoirs by writers of the 1980s, and hope to understand the literary ecology of the 1980s in this way. Here, we need to consider the following questions.

The first is why memoirs were written and published. As far as the official purpose is concerned, it is mainly to collect and organize historical materials for analysis and research, and to develop socialist literature and art. When it comes to individual writers, their approaches vary greatly. Some defend themselves or clear the names of others, while others record the times, reflect on history, recount their experiences, or express their suffering and highlight their character. Memoir writing is not only a manifestation of the Party and government's efforts to rectify the situation in the new era, but also an effort by writers to re-enter history and gain a place in literary history in the new historical time and space.

The next question is which writers need or can publish memoirs. In the early 1980s, it was mainly left-wing writers who were able to publish their memoirs, and those who needed to publish their memoirs were writers who had been wrongly criticized in history; in the late 1980s, with the change in the concept of literary history, the memoirs of non-left-wing writers with important literary and historical significance were also published.

In the end, the memoirs of writers could be written about whatever the writers wanted to write about. For ideological reasons, not all memoirs can be published; because of their own image, there are some important historical facts that writers do not want to recall, or that they deliberately distort to varying degrees when recalling them. This not only involves the literary ecology of the 1980s, but also reflects the ideology of a generation of writers in their twilight years.

The above is only a preliminary consideration of the significance, current status and possible research in this field before we go into an in-depth explanation of the memoirs of writers of the 1980s. Perhaps, with the further deepening of the research, some of the contents will be revised or even denied, and some new contents will also enter our research field. We are looking forward to the emergence of new historical materials and achievements in this field.

The Meaning of Historicization and Its Possibilities

-A Discussion on the Academic Trend of "Historicizing Contemporary Literature"[1]

"The historicization of contemporary literature" is a common concern in the academic world. This kind of "historicization" pursues an objective and neutral academic position, hoping to analyze the "aesthetic," "artistic," and "literary" aspects of writers' works in the specific historical context and to grasp their significance in literary history. The key to this problem lies in the controversy over the disciplinary, temporal and contemporary nature of contemporary literary research. In the process of research, these problems can be solved. In the specific promotion of "historicization", we can start with the basic historical materials, compile a collection of writers' works and historical books, and continue to research the contemporary literary system.

I. Defining the Concept of "Historicization of Contemporary Literature"

In recent years, the "historicization of contemporary literature" has become a focal point of general concern in the academic world. This can be clearly seen from the center of attention of famous scholars of contemporary literature and the themes of some academic conferences. In recent years, Hong Zicheng, Cheng Guangwei, Wu Xiuming, Wu Jun, and others have published a series of papers, books, or series of historical materials on the "historicization of contemporary literature", among which the more influential ones are Hong Zicheng's *The Concept of Contemporary Literature*,

---

1 Some scholars believe that this "historicizing" tendency in contemporary literary research is "more accurately summarized by 'academic turn' and 'academic trend' than by 'academic deepening'. It is because this 'historicization' of contemporary literary research and literary history writing is not a 'turn' at all, but a 'deepening'." Chen Jianhui, "Contemporary Literary Discipline Construction and Literary History Writing," Literary Review, No. 4, 2018.

Problems and Approaches: Lecture Notes on the History of Contemporary Literature in China, *Materials and Annotations*, and *The History of My Reading*, as well as the works of Cheng Guangwei and his disciples' *Returning to the 1980s*, *Collecting and Arranging Literary Historical Documents of the 1980s*, Wu Xiuming's series of articles explaining the academic methodology of "Historicization of Contemporary Literature", and his edited volume "Series of Historical Documents on Contemporary Chinese Literature", and Wu Jun's *Chronicle of Contemporary Chinese Literary Criticism*, among others.

Starting from "History of Contemporary Chinese Literature: Historical Concepts and Methods" and "Seminar on the Historicization of Contemporary Literary Studies" in 2007, the " Historicization of Contemporary Literature" has been very popular, especially in the past two years, many academic conferences related to contemporary literature have been related to "historicization" or "Historical documentation", such as "Contemporary Literature Historical Materials Research Center and Academic Symposium" in 2016, "Problems and Methods: Research on Chinese Contemporary Literary Historical Materials and Literary History' Academic Symposium" and "China Contemporary Literary Historical Materials Summit Forum" in 2017, "Construction and Research of Chinese Contemporary Literary Historical Materials' Academic Seminar" in 2018, "Academic Seminar on 'Historicization of Contemporary Chinese Literature'" in 2019, and so on. For this academic trend, which has been in existence for more than a decade but has been growing stronger rather than weakening, it is necessary to conduct a brief academic review.

Although the academic initiative of "historicization of contemporary literature" has been going on for ten years and so many scholars have actively participated in it, it seems that scholars do not have a unified understanding of the specific connotation of "historicization". According to Luo Changqing and Wu Xu's research, in the field of contemporary literary research, the specific meaning of "historicization" consists approximately of four aspects: literary creation, literary research, literary history compilation and disciplinary education. In literary creation, "historicization" refers to the expropriation of historical themes by writers and the borrowing of new historicist methods of creation; in literary research, "historicization" refers to the trend of "historiography" in the field of contemporary literary research; [1]in the codification of literary history, it implies a "rewriting" of contemporary literary history; and in disciplinary education, "historicization" advocates the legitimacy, stability and scholarship of contemporary literary disciplines.[2] In fact, there are two aspects in general, one is literary creation, let's leave it aside for the moment. The other is academic research. Whether it is the compilation of contemporary literary history or the construction of the discipline, they are both based on the study of contemporary literature.

The study of contemporary literature, which is directed towards the compilation of literary history and the building of disciplines, must break away from the tendency to focus purely on literary criticism, and this is probably where the meaning of the "historicization of contemporary literature" is to be found.

Cheng Guangwei is one of the most important scholars who advocate the "historicization of contemporary literature", and in the first few years, he has explained the concept of "historicization" many times. In his article "Historicization of the Contemporary Literary Discipline", he argues that "the

1 In the article "Historicizing" or "Historicizing": New Trends in the Study of Modern and Contemporary Chinese Literature (Chinese Modern Literature Research Series, No. 2, 2018), Qian Wenliang argues that the tendency of Chinese modern literary research since the 1990s is "too simplistic" to be summarized by "historicization", and "it would be better to adopt the postmodern sense of 'historicization'." "Instead, it is more practical and accurate to adopt the postmodern sense of 'historicization'.

2 Luo Changqing and Wu Xu, "The Concept of 'Historicization' in Contemporary Chinese Literature in the Perspective of Academic Phenomena", Proceedings of the Symposium on Historicization in Contemporary Chinese Literature, unpublished.

'historicization' of the contemporary literary discipline" refers to the 'sifting' through literary criticism, anthologies and classrooms". In his article "The Historicization of Contemporary Literature", he argues that "the 'historicization' of contemporary literature refers to the fact that the works of authors that have been 'screened' by literary criticisms, anthologies, and classrooms are 'past' literary facts, and that such work undoubtedly produces historical adequacy. That is to say, in the process of 'historicization' of the contemporary literary discipline, 'creation' and 'criticism' no longer represent the subjectivity of contemporary literature, they are in the same position with magazines, events, controversies, modes of production and literary systems, and have been deposited as several 'parts' of contemporary literary history, one of the many parallel but related components".[1] Later, in a conversation with his student Yang Qingxiang, he again mentioned "historicization". He pointed out: "By 'historicization', I do not mean the kind of macroscopic work that can effectively deal with all literary phenomena, but a very specific kind of work that emphasizes the researcher's personal historical experience, cultural memory and traumatic experience as a base, and then adds 'personal understanding' and fully respects the historical status of the writer and the work."[2] In the last few years, Cheng Guangwei's main work has been "collecting and organizing literature and documents on the history of literature in the 1980s", and he has not specifically elaborated and revised this concept, but we can see from his work that his understanding of this concept has not changed much.

In this academic concept, which is more rationalized and consciously aware of its theoretical limitations, we feel that there are two aspects worth thinking about. First, the status of the writer's work seems to be poorly

1 Cheng Guangwei, "The Historicization of Contemporary Literary Science", Literary Studies, No. 4, 2008.
2 Cheng Guangwei: The 'Historicization" of Contemporary Literature, Peking University Press, 2011, p. 232.

positioned. In the first concept, he thinks that "creation" and "criticism" are no longer the main body of contemporary literature, but only "one of the many components". This kind of research idea may fall back into the criticisms of Hong Zicheng's A History of Contemporary Chinese Literature. "In The History of Contemporary Chinese Literature, we can see neither classic writers nor classic works, and even the 'best' are hard to find."[1] Therefore, later on, he made necessary corrections, that is, "fully respect the historical status of writers and works". Secondly, the reference to "the researcher's individual historical experience" probably emphasizes the limitations of theory itself. But will the inclusion of this personal historical experience affect the realization of the goal of "historicization"? After all, "'historicization does not only mean 'historicizing' the subject, more importantly, it should also mean 'historicizing' the self."[2] The so-called "self-historicization" is to place one's own interpretation of history in a specific historical context, and to examine why one would have such an outlook in that context. The inclusion of the researcher's personal experience is inevitable, but we should always be wary of the essentialization of personal experience.

In this sense, we believe that the so-called "historicization of contemporary literature" can be roughly understood as placing the writers and works of contemporary literature in a specific historical context, applying the methods of intellectual archaeology, collecting and organizing relevant historical materials and facts, constructing the historical field of contemporary literary production and development through the close reading of texts and evaluating and measuring the historical value of specific writers and works within this field. In this field, it evaluates and measures the historical value of specific writers and works. It is not only concerned with the "aesthetic," "artistic,"

1 Chen Jianhui: "The Construction of Contemporary Literary Disciplines and the Writing of Literary History", Literary Review, No. 4, 2018.
2 Li Yang, Reinterpretation of Chinese Literary Classics in the 50s and 70s, Peking University Press, 2018, p. 357.

and "literary" analysis of specific works, but also wishes to place such analysis in the context of contemporary history in order to grasp their literary-historical significance in a certain historical period. It should be pointed out that this kind of historicization is not only a kind of academic pursuit, but also a kind of academic ideal, with an idealistic color. All history is contemporary history. Although we can try our best to maintain the objective and neutral academic standpoint in the process of academic research, it is undeniable that any rewriting of history is a dialog between "the present" and "history", and it is unrealistic for us to totally reject the idea that "the present" has influence on "history". The participation of the "present" in the work of "historicization" is fundamentally not only impossible to deny, but should also be a valuable stance upheld by all humanities and academic research. Moreover, by "historicization", we mean that we try our best to examine the object of our research in the historical context of contemporary literature at the level of consciousness.

II. The Controversial Focus of "Historicization of Contemporary Literature"

The reason why "the historicization of contemporary literature" has become a problem, the controversy mainly focuses on three points: the legitimacy of the subject, the temporality and the "contemporaneity". Why do some scholars spend so much effort on the historicization of contemporary literature? One important reason is that the identity of contemporary literature is questionable to many scholars. Not to mention Tang Tao's famous assertion that "it is not appropriate to write history in contemporary literature". Many years later, Xie Mian even put forward the idea that "now I advocate the abolition of contemporary literature."[1]"Contemporary literature is still 'unidentified' and its identity is very much in doubt. Undoubtedly,

1 Xiao Min and Li Yanwen, "A Review of the Academic Conference on the History of Contemporary Chinese Literature: Historical Concepts and Methods," Literature and Art Controversy, No. 12, 2007.

Contemporary Literature is a young subject in an 'unfinished' state, and it is also a subject with the least consensus, the most controversy, and the least satisfaction.[1] This state of the discipline of contemporary literature has made many scholars engaged in the study of contemporary literature feel uneasy. In this academic context, the proposal of "historicizing contemporary literature" is in itself an appeal to the legitimacy. In their view, "when a discipline develops to a certain point, the problem of 'historicization' is often raised"[2]. "The 'historicization' orientation of contemporary literary history writing is conducive to the stability and certainty of the discipline, and it can also make contemporary literary history closer to historical reality and more academic depth."[3]

The so-called temporal problem refers to the existence time of contemporary literature on the one hand, and its cut-off time and the sense of "historical distance" between the researcher and the object of study on the other. Advocates and supporters of the "historicization of contemporary literature" have repeatedly raised the question of the duration of contemporary literature, "Contemporary literature has a history of nearly sixty years, which is already twice as long as the duration of modern literature. Does it 'forever' remain in the state of 'criticism' without its own task of 'historicization'?"[4] "The problem of contemporary writing history has been talked about from the early 1980s to the present. What is strange is that no one has accused Zhu Ziqing and Zhou Zuoren of writing a treatise on the history of new literature at a time when new literature had been born for only a decade or so, but at a time

---

1 Chen Jianhui, "The Construction of Contemporary Literary Disciplines and the Writing of Literary History", Literary Review, No. 4, 2018.
2 Cheng Guangwei and Xia Xia, "Historical Data and Genealogy of Contemporary Writers: An Interview with Mr. Cheng Guangwei", New Literature Review, No. 1, 2018.
3 Chen Jianhui: "The Construction of Contemporary Literary Disciplines and the Writing of Literary History", Literary Review, No. 4, 2018.
4 Cheng Guangwei, "Historicization of Contemporary Literary Disciplines", Literary Studies, No. 4, 2008.

when contemporary literature has already passed 30, 40 or 60 years, they still say that it is too close to the time, and say that it is not possible to write a history. How many years does it take to be 'not too close'? The shortcomings of contemporary history written by contemporary people naturally exist, and there are many problems, but there are also some things that cannot be replaced by intergenerational or intersubgenerational stories told by contemporary people."[1]In such a sense to talk about "the historicization of contemporary literature", it is difficult for anyone to raise any objection. However, the key to the temporal problem may not lie here, but in the fact that "'Contemporary literature' does not yet have a clear temporal limit, and the researcher who is in the midst of it lacks the sense of historical distance that is necessary for objective and calm academic research and judgment."[2] Here, Gao Yuanbao, like many scholars who disagree with the "historicization of contemporary literature", equates "contemporary literature" with "literature of the present day". In fact, "literature of the present day" belongs to "contemporary literature", but "contemporary literature" is not equal to "literature of the present day". If "literature of the present day" cannot be historicized due to a lack of "necessary historical sense" among researchers, then what about "1980s literature," "Cultural Revolution literature," and "17-year literature," which are already 30, 40, and 50 years away from us? When Tang Tao proposed that "it is not appropriate to write a history of contemporary literature", it was mainly because he understood "contemporary literature" as "literature of the present day". "Our contemporary literature, counting from the founding of the People's Republic of China, encompasses more than thirty years of history. Does it mean that the literature of thirty years ago is still the

---

1 Wei Peina: "The Illness of 'Literary History,' the 'Myth of the Century'—An Interview with Hong Zicheng, Professor of Chinese Literature at Peking University and Scholar of Contemporary Chinese Literature," Shenzhen Commercial Daily, September 15, 2014.

2 Gao Yuanshao: "The 'Historicization' Trend in the Study of Chinese Modern and Contemporary Literature," Journal of Chinese Modern Literature Studies, No. 2, 2017.

current literature, and the literature of the 1950s is still the current literature in the 1980s? It is more appropriate to categorize these into the scope of modern literature. In other words, they are no longer literature of the present day, they can be regarded as historical materials, and should be recorded in the history books." [1]

As we can see from Tang Tao's words, at that time, he did not object to the inclusion of the "literature of the fifties" in the history books, not to mention that more than 30 years have passed since then. In this sense, we think that, like Hong Zicheng's study of "seventeen years literature" and Cheng Guangwei's study of "eighties' literature", we should select a certain historical period to "fix them down" and conduct a historical study to carry out the work of historicization. This is completely possible.

After solving the problem of temporality, the problem of "contemporaneity" will not be difficult to solve. The reason why some scholars disagree with the "historicization of contemporary literature" is that they cherish the "contemporaneity" of contemporary literature, believing that "contemporaneity is essential to the study and criticism of contemporary literature. It is the fundamental attribute of 'contemporary literature', 'contemporary literary research' and 'contemporary literary criticism' that must be upheld. [2]Contemporary literary studies "must always be kept in the perspective of the present, and it is only in their connection with the present that they can become the content of contemporary literary history"[3]. This valuing of "contemporaneity" reflects the scholars' defense of the social function of

---

1 Tang Tao, "Contemporary Literature Should Not Write History," Contemporary Literary Thoughts, No. 3, 1982.

2 Zhang Qinghua, "Between Historicization and Contemporaneity - Reflections on the State of Contemporary Literary Research and Criticism", Literary Studies, No. 12, 2009.
3 Liu Fusheng, "Historicization and Anti-Historicization", Proceedings of the Academic Symposium on Historicization in Contemporary Chinese Literature, unpublished.

contemporary literary research. What they fear is that the "historicization of contemporary literature" may lead the study of contemporary literature further towards academization and bibliolatry, thus weakening the social function of contemporary literary research. This is an invaluable spiritual responsibility of humanities scholars. However, in terms of academic research, if we recognize that "contemporary literature" includes not only "literature of the present day" but also literature that is more than 30 years away from us, then, conducting historical research on this part of literature probably won't damage the valuable quality of "contemporaneity," right? Although we agree with the historical judgment that "the eighties have not passed away, they are still our direct present."[1] We feel that it would be a bit too obsessive to oppose the historical study of the "literature of the eighties" on this basis. If this is the case, how should we judge the historicization of modern literature? Has the "May Fourth" passed? In fact, the "historicization of contemporary literature" does not necessarily lead to the weakening of "contemporaneity". All history is contemporary history, and a good scholar, even in the study of ancient literature, is bound to be concerned with the history of the present. What is more, the main body of contemporary literary research is still literary criticism.

From this, we think that contemporary literature should be historicized and can be historicized, but the key question is how to historicize it.

III. "Historicization of Contemporary Literature" and Related Work

Specifically, how should the work of historicization be carried out?

The fundamental work is, of course, the collection and organization of historical documents. "Without the foundation of documentation, the 40 years of research on the new period of literature may always remain in the

1 Liu Fusheng, "Historicization and Anti-Historicization", Proceedings of the Academic Symposium on "Historicization in Contemporary Chinese Literature", n.d.

stage of 'raising questions', and it is impossible to turn the many questions we have thought into concrete research and carry out the study step by step, deeper and deeper."[1]This is the case for New Age literature, and even more so for Contemporary Literature. At present, the main documents that have been compiled include: *Research Materials on Chinese Contemporary Literature* published by Guizhou People's Publishing House in the 1980s, *Compilation of Research Materials on Chinese Literature in the New Period* edited by Kong Fanjin, Lei Da, Wu Yiqin, etc., *Historical Materials of Literature in the New Period and Catalog of Contemporary Literature of China* edited by Cheng Guangwei, *Historical Materials of Chinese Contemporary Literature Series* edited by Wu Xiuming, *Historical Series of Chinese Contemporary Literature* edited by Wu Jun, *Research Materials Series on Jiangsu Contemporary Writers* edited by Ding Fan, Wang Bibin, Wang Yao, and Zhu Xiaojin, *Research Materials Series of the Central China Plains Writers' Groups* edited by Cheng Guangwei, Wu Shengang, and Shen Wenhui, etc. These historical materials and documents have been widely recognized by the Chinese writers' groups. These historical documents are mainly about writers' works, literary thinking trends, literary genres, literary styles, literary periodicals and so on in the history of contemporary Chinese literature. They are very important historical materials for the study of the historicization of contemporary Chinese literature. Among them, *the Catalogue of Contemporary Chinese Literature Periodicals* edited by Cheng Guangwei, and *the Chronicle of Critical History of Contemporary Chinese Literature edited* by Wu Jun are of great significance. They are a cataloging endeavor of contemporary Chinese literary journals, and a fundamental historical source for the history of contemporary Chinese literary criticism.

---

1 Cheng Guangwei, "How to Study the Literature of the New Period", Contemporary Writers' Review, No. 5, 2018.

These two works are the first of their kind in the study of contemporary Chinese literary history.

From this, we can also realize that in the work of historicizing contemporary Chinese literature, we can't always do repetitive work around a few writers and a few currents of thought.

In fact, there are still many issues related to historical materials that need to be further resolved. The first issue is the compilation of the Dictionary of Contemporary Chinese Literature. Dictionaries related to ancient and modern literature have already been created and have had a considerable impact, such as the Encyclopedia of Chinese Writers compiled by Tan Zhengbi, the Dictionary of Chinese Literature edited by Qian Zhonglian and others, and the Dictionary of Modern Chinese Literature edited by Jia Zhifang and others. In terms of contemporary Chinese literature, there is the New Chinese Literary Dictionary edited by Pan Xulan, but it was published in 1993, which was more than 20 years ago. Its revision or recodification should be emphasized. The second is the compilation of bibliographic summaries of contemporary Chinese literature. In the history of modern Chinese literature, there are a number of influential bibliographic works, such as The General Bibliography of Modern Chinese Literature, edited by Jia Zhifang and Yu Yuangui, The Compendium of Periodical Catalogues of Modern Chinese Literature, edited by Tang Yuan and others, The Summary of the General Catalogues of Modern Chinese Drama, edited by Dong Jian, and The Summary of Chinese Novels (Modern Part), edited by Guo Qizong and others. In contemporary literature, there have been some such works, such as The Abstract of Chinese Contemporary Drama, edited by Dong Jian and Lu Wei, and The Catalogue of Chinese Contemporary Literature Periodicals, edited by Cheng Guangwei, but similar works have not yet appeared in other disciplines. Compared with modern literature, contemporary literature has a longer time span, more writers and works, and is always in the process of development, so it is a fact that it is more difficult to organize and write such a large-scale tool book. However, the difficulty is not insurmountable. If it is difficult to tackle contemporary literature as a whole, can we focus on completing a specific time period first? For example, *Literature of the Seventeen Years*, *Literature of the Cultural Revolution*, *Literature of the Eighties*, etc. The second issue is how to collect and organize historical materials related to contemporary literary "public cases."

In the history of contemporary Chinese literature, there are a lot of famous "public cases", such as the series of literary criticisms in the period of "seventeen years", the debates on various literary trends in the 1980s and even the controversy surrounding *The Waste City* in the early 1990s. To a certain extent, a history of contemporary literary controversy is a history of contemporary literary development. If we can fully excavate and organize the various archival materials behind each controversy, it will be a great contribution to the historicization of contemporary literature. Such work has already been done, such as the "Historical Archives Book Series" edited and published by the School of Literature of Shandong Normal University, and *the New Period Literary Historical Materials Series* edited by Cheng Guangwei, which deals with important literary trends such as the literature of traumas, the literature of reflection, and the Misty poetry, but it is not the same as the historical data collection of the "public case". More often than not, they treat these phenomena as a trend of thought, and the historical materials they collect are more research papers about them. If they were to be treated as "public cases", more relevant historical information would have to be gathered to show their origin and development. Of course, there are many difficulties in doing so, including the confidentiality of the archives and the writers' personnel. The final issue is related to writers' memoirs, including oral histories. The value of writers' memoirs has not yet been fully recognized in the history of modern and contemporary Chinese literature. We now mainly use them as supporting materials whose authenticity has yet to be verified. In fact, they play a very important role in the revision of authors' chronicles and the writing of biographies. The value of these documents cannot be underestimated, even for the study and rewriting of a literary history. In the 1980s, for example, "Writing memoirs is an important way for many old writers [1]to return to the literary world, and it should also be an indispensable page in the literary history of the 1980s. These memoirs provide us with the 'other half' of the 1980s literature, which has been seriously neglected: a different literary pattern, literary trend, literary ecology and the spiritual personality of the writers in the 1980s. They not only have an indispensable historical position in the non-fiction writing of the 1980s, but also provide us with the possibility of sketching the mental state of these writers in the twilight of their lives as a whole. At a time when more and more attention is being paid to the construction of contemporary literary history, the historical organization, documentary examination, and comprehensive study of the memoirs of writers in the 1980s can not only provide us with a new perspective of 'back to the 1980s', but also provide historical support for future studies of modern and contemporary literature"[2]. If some writers are unable to write their memoirs for various reasons, should we consider collaborating with them to create oral histories? This would be both a convenient option and an urgent task for contemporary literary studies.

For the classicization of a writer and the historicization of a literary period, a fundamental work is the collection, arrangement and publication of a

---

1 The "old writers" in this context refer to those writers who have been important in the literary world since the May Fourth Movement and who are still alive in the 1980s and have published their memoirs in various forms, such as Mao Dun, Bajin, Hu Feng, Ding Ling, Bing Xin, Xia Yian, Zang Kejia, Yang Han-Shen, Xu Mou-Yong, Chen Bai-Dan, Zhao Jia-Bi, Xu Jie, Wang Xiyan, and so on. They include Mao Dun, Ba Jin, Hu Feng, Ding Ling, Bing Xin, Xia Yan, Zang Ke Jia, Yang Han Si, Xu Maoyong, Chen Baichan, Zhao Jiabi, Xu Jie, and Wang Xiyan. Reference note.

2 Xu Hongjun, "The Significance, Present Situation and Possibilities of the Study of Writers' Memoirs in the 1980s", Tianfu Xinjian, No. 4, 2018.

collection of writers' works. In the history of ancient literature, we have *All the Ancient Three Dynasties, Qin, Han, Three Kingdoms, and Six Dynasties*, *Poetry of the Pre-Qin, Wei, Jin, and Southern and Northern Dynasties*, *All Tang Dynasty Poetry*, *All Song Dynasty Prose*, *All Song Dynasty Poetry*, *All Song Dynasty Lyrics* and other works of all dynasties and collections of writers such as *Complete Collection of Li Taibai*; in the history of modern literature, we have t*he New Chinese Literature Series* and other collections of works of specific period, and *Complete Works of Lu Xun*, *The Complete Works of Guo Moruo*, *The Complete Works of Mao Dun*, *The Complete Works of Ba Jin*, *The Complete Works of Lao She*, *The Collected Works of Cao Yu*, *The Collected Works of Shen Congwen*, and other famous writers' collections. Under these premises, the historicization of ancient and modern Chinese literature has been able to continue to advance steadily. Compared with the ancient and modern literature, the research of contemporary Chinese literature seems to pay more attention to the writers' collections. At present, the collected works of those writers who had a great influence on the literature of "17 years" have been published in a comprehensive manner, such as Zhou Yang's *Collected Works*, *the complete works of Hu Feng*, *the Complete Works of Ding Ling*, *the Complete Works of Feng Xuefeng*, *the Complete Works of Xia Yan*, *the Complete Works of Zhao Shuli*, *He Jingzhi's Collected Works*, *the Complete Works of Sun Li*, *Liu Qing's Collected Works*, and *Yang Mo's Collected Works*, etc. *The Collected Works of the New Era Writers* have been published in a steady manner. The work of compiling and publishing the collections of writers in the new era was relatively complicated. After the death of some writers, their collections were gradually published through various efforts, such as *Zeng Zhuo's Collected Works*, *Lv Yuan' Collected Works*, *Niu Han's Collected Poems*, *Dai Houying's Collected Works*, *Gao Xiaosheng's Collected Works*, the *Complete Poetry of Hai Zi*, *the complete Poetry of Gu Cheng*, *Yao Xueyin's Collected Works*, *Xu Chi's Collected Works*, *the Complete Works of Lu Yao*, *Lin Jinlan's Collected Works* and *the Complete*

Works of Wang Zengqi, etc. The publication of these anthologies will play a very important role in establishing these writers as classics and in historicizing the literature of the 1980s. However, there are still a lot of important writers who have passed away and whose anthologies have not yet been organized and published, such as Ru Zhijuan, Zhang Yiyong, Zhou Keqin, Zhang Xianliang, Wang Runzhi, Shi Tiesheng, Wang Xiaobo, and so on.

The scattered and incomplete nature of the works will have a certain impact on the overall study of the writer and on the overall advancement of a period of literary history. Compared with the dead authors, the compilation and publication of the collected works of the living authors may be more troublesome. For one thing, many writers are still in the process of creating, and the authority of their collections may be questioned under such circumstances. For example, after Mo Yan won the Nobel Prize for Literature in 2012, Writers' Publishing House and Yunnan People's Publishing House released the 20-volume Collected Writings of Mo Yan at almost the same time. This behavior is more like a commercial operation than an academic summary. After Shaanxi People's Publishing House published the 18-volume Collected Writings of Jia Pingwa in 1998, Shanghai Literature and Art Publishing House published the 20-volume Collected Writings of Jia Pingwa in 2013. It does not mean that after a publishing house publishes a certain author's collection, other publishing houses cannot publish it again, but rather, if a writer is still in the period of vigorous literary creation, the publication of such a collection will probably be a waste of academic resources. In contrast, the 2019 edition of *The Complete Works of Wang Zengqi* by the People's Literature Publishing House is much more valuable. Although the Beijing Normal University Publishing House published the complete works of Wang Zengqi one year after his death (1998), it is clear that the work of the People's Literature Publishing House was more solid and comprehensive 20 years later, and will provide a more authoritative historical basis for the advancement of Wang Zengqi's research. Another reason for the difficulty of publishing the collected works of living writers is probably related to the writers themselves. Since many writers are still in a creative mode, they may not be willing to release their collections in the process. This requires a consensus between writers and scholars. Generally speaking, in the process of "historicizing contemporary literature", we should pay full attention to the collection and publication of writers' works.

With the joint efforts of several generations of scholars, the New Literature Series of China has been in the process of finalizing the edition. This work will certainly have a significant impact on the historicization of contemporary Chinese literature. However, it seems that their value has not yet been fully recognized. As far as the organization and publication of writers' collections are concerned, it needs the support of the academic evaluation system, as well as the active cooperation of the writers and their families.

The third aspect of the "Historicization of Contemporary Literature" is the compilation of writers' genealogies, biographies and writers' theories. At a sharing session for the release of the new book in the series On Contemporary Chinese Writers, Wu Yi-qin pointed out that "Theory of Writers" is a tradition in the study of contemporary Chinese literature, and also represents the highest level of modern literary research, and it can be said that all the works that have been repeatedly read and cited by scholars for generations are actually "Theory of Writers". It can be said that the works that have been repeatedly read and quoted by generations of scholars in the study of modern literature are in fact all 'Writers' Theory'." "In the field of contemporary writers, we are obviously inadequate, and most of the studies on contemporary literature are on-the-spot commentaries and tracking studies, while systematic and comprehensive studies are weak."[1] In the study of ancient and modern Chinese literature, many scholars started their academic career from the study of a specific writer, or became famous for their study of a specific writer. For example, Yuan Xingpei's study of Tao Yuanming, Mo Lifeng's study of Du Fu, Qian Liqun's and Wang Furen's study of Lu Xun, Chen Sihe and Li Hui's study of Ba Jin, Ling Yu's study of Shen Congwen, and Chen Xiaoming's study of Sha Ding and Ai Wu, etc. In the field of contemporary literature, such phenomena are still relatively rare.

Since contemporary literature lacks such classic writers, "it is not worth" spending so much effort. As far as "Seventeen years" literature is concerned, since there are more "single book writers", they may not be able to withstand this kind of research, but the value of Yang Mo, Liu Qing and other writers has yet to be fully recognized. If we count from the Fourth Literature Congress in 1978, new period literature has a history of more than 40 years. In these 40 years, many important writers have emerged, such as Wang Zengqi, Lu Yao, Wang Xiaobo, Shi Tiesheng, Chen Zhongshi, Gu Cheng, Hai Zi, Mo Yan, Wang Meng, Jia Ping Au, Wang Anyi, Han Shaogong, Zhang Chengzhi, Liu Zhenyun, Zhang Wei, Yu Hua, Zhang Jie, Fang Fang, etc. To a certain extent, these writers represent the most important writers of the New Period. To a certain extent, these writers represent the achievements of Chinese literature since the New Era. In the process of promoting "contemporary literary history", in order to make the study of contemporary literature truly "de-criticized", the chronicles, biographies, and theories of these writers are in fact an indispensable task. On this point, the "Writers' Genealogy Column" opened by Dongwu Academic embodies a kind of forward-looking academic research. Starting from 2012, Dongwu Academic has published the literary annals of Su Tong, A Lai, Yu Hua, Han Shaogong, Shi Tiesheng, Tie Ning,

1 Gao Kai, "Contemporary Chinese Writers' Discourse" series published, China News Network, https://baijiahao. baidu. com/ s? id =16098410514 26031543&wfr = spider&for = pc.

Zhai Yongming, Mo Yan, Wang Zengqi, Zhang Chengzhi, Jia Pingwa, Lin Bai, Li Peifu, Liu Zhenyun, Bi Feiyu, Chen Zhongshi, and Zhang Wei, etc. Later, it was published in the form of the Chronicles of Contemporary Famous Writers and Scholars series, which had a very good academic impact. In 2018, the first series of Chinese Contemporary Writers edited by famous critic Xie Youshun was published by Writers' Publishing House, including nine books, including A Cheng, Chang Yao, Ge Fei, Jia Pingwa, Lu Yao, Wang Meng, Wang Xiaobo, Yan Geling and Yu Hua. This foundational work will undoubtedly play a pivotal role in the process of "historicizing contemporary literature."

In addition to the construction of basic historical materials and the study of the historicization of writers' works, the historicization of contemporary literature should also include the knowledge cleansing of related concepts as well as the study of literary institutions, including literary institutions, literary journals, literary publications, literary conferences, literary awards, and so on. Hong Zicheng's achievements are the most prominent in the intellectual cleaning-up of contemporary literature. As early as the 1990s, he began to work on this consciously. "In our past literary history, how were the facts, concepts, and evaluations that we often used and were unaware of formed, and by what methods were they 'constructed'? - This was my main thinking in the 1990s." "Through this kind of 'cleaning-up', cracks can be exposed in the narratives that appeared to be very tight and unified in the past, and errors and cracks can be found in the overall board, the 'board' that appeared to be very smooth and smoothed out by words. It is possible to find mistakes and cracks in the 'block' that seems to be smooth and smoothed out by words, and then to reveal the contradictions and discrepancies in the narrative. This method is to find problems in the conclusions of an existing narrative or, rather, to use the 'end point' of an existing narrative as the 'beginning point' of its emergence."[1] His work in this regard is highlighted in his History of Contemporary Chinese Literature, Materials and Notes, as well as in his work on "Contemporary Literature", "Left-Wing Literature", "Subject Matter", "Sample", "Crafts", etc. Among the young scholars, Luo Changqing of Guizhou Normal University is the one who has made more efforts to clean up the knowledge of contemporary literature, and his achievements are also more outstanding. Since 2010, he has been working on "Red Army Women's Corps", "The Red Lanterns", "Literature of the Underclass", "New Century Literature", "Contemporary Chinese Literature", "Seventeen Years Literature" and other literary materials, critical concepts and concepts of literary history have been persistently cleaned up, revealing to us the history of many literary concepts and the historical background behind them.

"Chinese socialist literature is a new type of literature unprecedented in history. In order to ensure the socialist nature of literature, to maintain the leading position of socialist culture, and to cooperate with and promote the socialist political and economic construction, it has gradually established a set of management mechanisms for literary organization, guidance and evaluation, which we call the literary system."[2]A significant difference between contemporary literature and ancient literature and modern literature is that contemporary literature, especially the literature before the 1980s, is closely related to the management system of the state and has a very obvious institutionalized characteristic. Therefore, the study of the contemporary literary system has been the concern of many scholars. The representative results of this field include: Wang Benzhao and Zhang Jun's studies on the contemporary literary system, Fan Guoying's and Ren Donghua's studies on Mao Dun

---

1 Hong Zicheng: "Problems and Methods: Lectures on the Study of Chinese Contemporary Literary History", Life - Reading - Xinzhi Sanlian Bookstore, 2002, p. 89.
2 Wang Benzhao: Zhongguo Contemporary Literary System Research (1949~1976), New Star Publishing House, 2007, p. 1.

Literary Prize, Si Yanwei's and Wang Xiutao's studies on literary conferences, Xu Yong's studies on literary anthology, Wu Jun's and Huang Fayou's studies on People's Literature, Yan Gang, Zhang Jun and Wei Baotao's studies on Literary Arts Newspaper, Lian Min and Qian Jiyun's studies on Poetry Magazine, and Yang Yi Fei's studies on Morning Glory, and Gong Kui Lin's studies on "People's Daily Literary Supplement. Besides, there are some other issues related to the contemporary literary academic system that deserve attention. For example, in the history of contemporary Chinese literature, What literary institutions have had a significant influence? What impact have they had on the history of contemporary Chinese literature? The Chinese Writers' Association, the Central Institute of Literature[1], the Institute of Literature of Peking University[2], the People's Literature Publishing House, the Writers' Publishing House, the New Literature Publishing House[3], the China Youth Publishing House, and PLA Literature and Art, Wen Hui Magazine, People's Drama, Shanghai Literature, Harvest, Contemporary, Hua Cheng and October and other important literary journals, also have to be studied in depth and promoted. For example, there are very few results on contemporary literary editing, and the only ones that exist are generally not of a high level.

1 The Central Institute of Literature was founded in December 1950, and in July 1953 it was placed under the leadership of the Chinese Writers' Association and renamed the Literary Institute of the Chinese Writers' Association, which ceased to exist in November 1957, was restored in January 1980, and in November 1984 it was renamed the Institute of Lusheng Literature. At the time of the publication of the article, there was an error in the note, which was pointed out and corrected by Prof. Yuan Hongquan, for which we are grateful.

2 The Institute of Literature of Peking University was founded on February 22, 1953, renamed the Institute of Literature of the Department of Philosophy and Social Sciences of the Chinese Academy of Sciences in September 1955, and in 1977 it was renamed the Institute of Literature of the Chinese Academy of Social Sciences.

3 New Literature and Art Publishing House was renamed Shanghai Literature and Art Publishing House in 1952.

The above are merely our ideas regarding some fundamental historical research work, the "historicization of contemporary literature" is of course a very complex task, besides these historical materials, it also includes many equally important issues, such as the academic qualifications of literary historians, the selection and interpretation of contemporary literary classics, the evaluation of the achievements of contemporary literature, etc. These are all very important tasks, but they must be based on fundamental historical materials and may be even more controversial, so we will not repeat them here.

Originally published in Chinese Contemporary Literature Research, No. 5.

The above are merely our ideas regarding [illegible] historical research work, the transformation of [illegible] technology [illegible] very complex task [illegible] it is [illegible] quite important [illegible] the [illegible] qualifications [illegible] to further [illegible] selection [illegible] evaluation [illegible] these are all [illegible] fundamental [illegible]

[illegible]

Serie III New Century Literary Criticism

The Extreme Flower: Telling a Different Story after *Blind Mountain*

Jia Pingwa must have seen the movie *Blind Mountain*.

Although he told us in the afterword of The Extreme Flower that "this is a true story "[1], we still feel that from the beginning to the end, as well as the whole framework of the story, Hu Die and Bai Xuemei share so many similarities. From being deceived into working away from home to being trafficked to a rural area in northwest China, from repeated failed escape attempts to being raped and impregnated, especially the imagined methods of rescuing the female protagonist and the ending, all of this makes Extreme Flower seem like a mere textual retelling of Blind Mountain. Here, we do not want to doubt the "authenticity" of Hu Die's story, but we would like to discuss the possibility of innovation in the novel.

The ability to tell a story is crucial to a novelist. Although we have no doubt that Hu Die's story comes from that rainless summer "ten years ago", from the personal experience of the writer's hometown, but how to tell a story that differs from previous works about human trafficking should clearly be a question that writers give serious consideration to. When the story of Hu Die is almost the same as that of Bai Xuemei, can we say that the creativity of writers has not been fully demonstrated? Perhaps Jia Pingwa only heard the outline of the story of his fellow villager's daughter being trafficked. Due to his lack of life experience, he could only draw on his previous works to develop the narrative.

Even if it is only a story of women trafficking, Extreme Flower has its own value.

Lu Xun's brilliance lies in the fact that when others were calling on Chinese women to break through the bondage of feudal families, he asked the

---

1 Jia Pingwa, "Extreme Flowers - Postscript", People's Literature, No. 1, 2016.

question of "What will happen after Nora's runaway" on a more profound level. As an outstanding novelist, Jia Pingwa's reflections on social issues do not merely echo the opinions of others. As a story of trafficked women, the significance of "Extreme Flower" should be more reflected in its imagination of Hu Die's life after she was rescued: even if Hu Die was successfully rescued, could her life go back to the past?

Near the end of the story, Hu Die has a dream. After being rescued and returned to the city, what she faced was no happier than what she'd experienced in Geliang village, and it was even worse. The humiliation and hurt caused by the press interviews that appeared in her life in the face of social conscience was too much for her to bear: "I resented their questions, I felt like they were undressing me, humiliating me by stripping me naked." Instead of sympathizing with her sister's plight, her brother, who had dropped out of school to pay for her to continue her education, now felt "ashamed" that she had been trafficked. "You've got to be ashamed of yourself," he said. "Shame on you, and shame on me!" The people around her also had a cruel change in the way they looked at her: "In the alley, people came and went, when they suddenly saw me, all froze and gave me a silent smile, but then stopped and looked back." All this reminds readers of the Enlightenment novels of the May Fourth period, in which the criticism of human nature had found a more valuable entry point. If the writer really wants to "write a believable history of self-wrestling and restoration in the depths of human nature in the midst of the cycle of China's city and countryside" and "expose the dark side of human nature"[1], then the above should not be treated as a mere illusion, but should be given much more attention than it is given. Instead, much more space should have been spent on its detailed portrayal and

1 Ding Fan: "Jia Pingwa's Novel Extreme Flowers: A Chinese Urban-Rural 'Red and Black' Ink-wash Genre Painting," Literary News, February 3, 2016.

writing. However, Jia Pingwa has treated it as a dream, indicating that this was not the author's creative goal.

What is the author trying to say?

In fact, there are a thousand Hamlets in the eyes of a thousand readers. The story is not too long, less than 150,000 words, and the story is not too complicated, almost like *Blind Mountain*, which tells the story of a girl who was trafficked to the northwest countryside. For such a novel, there should not be much difference in the interpretation of its theme. In fact, although *Extreme Flower* has not been published for a long time, there are already two different opinions about the interpretation of its theme. One view, which we quoted in the previous section, is that it exposes the darkness of human nature. This viewpoint, because it focuses only on the abduction and sale of Hu Die, and takes the novel's detailed description of the Northwestern countryside as "endless chattering and rambling", unrelated to the theme. Another viewpoint is that it is "using this special reverse urbanization direction to express the author's concern for the people in the gap between urban and rural areas". [1]If the first view misinterprets the author's depiction of rural customs and folklore due to an excessive fixation on the theoretical premises of intellectual enlightenment, then the second view may overlook Hu Die's observations and experiences in Geliang Village by overly focusing on the "deurbanization dimension" of her "rural-urban-rural" journey. However, these elements occupy a significant portion of the novel and even surpass Hu Die's own story to some extent. This becomes clear when comparing Extreme Flowers with Blind Mountain.

Why do we have to compare *The Extreme Flower* with *Blind Mountain*? It is not only because they are very similar in terms of storytelling, but also because it allows us to see more clearly the creative goal of *The Extreme*

1 Gu Chao, "Jia Pingwa's 'Extreme Flower': Heavy Realistic Concerns", People's Daily, January 29, 2016.

Flower. If *Extreme Flower* is to focus on "people in the gap between urban and rural areas" through Hu Die's "reverse urbanization", or to expose the darkness of human nature through Hu Die's life experience, then the creation of *Extreme Flower* after *Blind Mountain* is a kind of meaningless repetition. In terms of "reverse urbanization", Hu Die, who dropped out of junior high school and went to the city to work, is far less significant than Bai Xuemei, who borrowed money to go to the city to study at the university, and then was tricked to a rural village in the Northwest after graduation; and in terms of exposing the darkness of human nature, *Blind Mountain* is far more intuitive and comprehensive than *Extreme Flowers*.

So, after *Blind Mountain*, why did Jia Pingwa write another long novel with a very similar plot?

Actually, rather than saying that *Extreme Flower* focuses on Hu Die, it would be more accurate to say that the author wants to use Hu Die's perspective and experiences to show us the desolation and sadness of rural northwest China.

The first-person protagonist narrative perspective is used in *Extreme Flower*, which through Hu Die's eyes not only tells the tragic experience of a girl being tricked into the Northwest countryside, but also shows us the backwardness and hardship of the Northwest countryside. Generally speaking, the narrative perspective of the first-person protagonist focuses more on telling the story of the protagonist herself, and this is even more true for Hu Die. When the life of a young girl in her flowering season takes a great turn, and her beautiful dream of life is confined overnight in a dark and cramped farmhouse, all her energy should be devoted to the change of her fate and the possibility of her next chance to escape, just like Bai Xuemei in *Blind Mountain*. However, in terms of the content of the novel, Hu Die tells more heartbreaking daily life of the people of Geliang village than her own story. It is through Hu Die's eyes that we see the monotony of the Hei liang family's three meals a day, the hard repetitions of their daily lives, and see the villagers' lack of economic resources, the difficulties men face in finding a wife, the boredom of their daily lives, the severity of natural disasters, the harshness of the living environment, the secretive majesty of the grand grandfather, the tragic fate of Aunt Mazi, and the pitiful and pathetic lives of Zi Mi, etc.... It can be said that Hu Die's concern for the outside world far exceeds her concern for her own fate. From the point of view of the first-person protagonist narrative and Hudie's life experiences, this is hard to understand. If there is an explanation for this phenomenon, which is difficult to explain in terms of narrative logic, it can only be the author's narrative position. Jia Pingwa said, "I really don't want to write it as a pure story of abduction of women and children", "I am concerned with how the city is getting fatter and how the countryside is withering away". In this novel, what he wants to do is not simply to tell a story of women trafficking, but to tell a story of the Northwest countryside from a folkloric standpoint with the help of Hu Die's eyes.

The narrative stance of Blind Mountain is one of the elite intellectuals, full of the impulse of enlightenment and a critical vision of reality. The ignorance and backwardness of Huang Degui and the villagers around him, the weakness and recognition of other women who have been trafficked here like Bai Xuemei, and the neglect and even prejudice against education in the whole countryside ... all make us think of the enlightenment novels of the May Fourth period. In addition to the enlightenment of thought, *Blind Mountain*, while telling the story of Bai Xuemei, also puts forward a harsh criticism of the cruel social reality. Huang Degui's brutal violence, the postman's loss of conscience, the indifference of the people around him, the local government's inaction, the police's failure to rescue, and Manager Wu's heartlessness, etc. are all accomplices in the formation of Bai Xuemei's tragedy. It seems more appropriate to summarize the theme of *Blind Mountain* with "concern for the people in the urban-rural gap" and "exposure of the dark side of human nature".

The narrative position of *The Extreme Flower* is closer to rural life. If *Blind Mountain* is an attempt to express the purpose of enlightenment and the power of criticizing reality through Bai Xuemei's life tragedy, then *Extreme Flower* is an attempt to show us, through Hu Die's eyes, the apoptosis and failure of the rural world in the process of China's rapid urbanization. If the tone of *Blind Mountain* is indignant and critical, then *Extreme Flower* is full of heartbreaking tears and helpless sighs of an intellectual standing in the position of a peasant.

The narrative stance of The Extreme Flower is mainly reflected in the following aspects:

First of all, the viewpoint of the main character, Hu Die, is not directed to herself, but more to the external rural world. It is not difficult to see the author's creative intention from the contradiction of the narrative logic: he does not want to repeat the story of women abduction in imitation of others, but he wants to tell the life demands of the Northwestern people with the help of such a story framework.

Secondly, the peasants in "Extreme Flower" are not the ignorant and mindless group that is enlightened and criticized, but the kind and poor villagers who are worthy of sympathy and help. Whether it is the Hei Liang family, or the great grandfather, Aunt Mazi, Zi Mi and others, they are all kind, full of goodwill and concern for Hu Die, and they are surviving humbly in the poor mountains and bad water of Geliang Village where they were born and will grow old in the end. In their living world, material resources are extremely scarce, and the only extreme flower is on the verge of extinction due to over-excavation, and Zi Mi and a few other women have to climb the rugged and bumpy snow-covered mountains in order to dig up the flower.

The townspeople's staple diet consisted of nothing but beans, and in order to offer Hu Die better meal, Hei Liang had to go to the town to buy white steamed buns. The extremely difficult living conditions make it difficult to attract women from outside the village, and the men of Geliang village have tried everything to get married and start a family. However, their efforts have not been rewarded. The majority of the men are still unable to find a wife. "The girls in the village are not willing to marry inward, and even the ones who have become daughters-in-law are running away from the village," "Over the years, the village population is getting smaller and smaller, but the number of bachelors is increasing". Faced with the helpless reality, the bachelors in the village asked Hei Liang's father to make woman-shaped stone sculptures, hoping that this can bring good luck to themselves, or at least can comfort their lonely souls. "Those unmarried men who hadn't yet found wives gave names to all the stones in the village. They determined which stone woman belonged to whom based on their size, height, and shape. The men would often go and touch them, rubbing the stones until their faces turned black and super shiny." These saddening and helpless details are by no means "repetitive, rambling customs and trivialities", but rather a deep sympathy and realistic accusation full of the writer's pain and tears.

Again, Hu Die gradually finds her identity in Geliang village. In the movie *Blind Mountain*, Bai Xuemei is always hostile to the village where she was abducted. At the end of the movie, when the former police officer who came to rescue her asks her if she wants to go back, Bai Xuemei replies angrily, "I will go back even if I die! They are animals, not human beings!" Her words were filled with criticism and accusations. Unlike Bai Xuemei, Hu Die gradually realized her own identity in Geliang Village. At first, Hu Die is another Bai Xuemei, filled with anger and resistance to the fact that she has been abducted. Her cries of "I want to go back" and "I want to go back to the city" express Hu Die's struggle against her fate. However, Hu Die's thoughts changed gradually, and in the end, she consciously gave up waiting for her mother and returned to the village. Of course, there were many frustrations along the way, and giving up and fleeing nearly drained her of all her strength. "I had no weight, no body, the more I walked, the more I became a piece of paper, the wind blew me to stick to the wall of the kiln here, and then to the wall of the kiln over there". This sense of helpless acceptance of fate is vastly different from the fierce struggle depicted in *Blind Mountain*.

There is an interesting phenomenon, in the first few parts of the novel, Hu Die is still telling the details of the marks she carved on the kiln wall with her fingernails, which is to calculate the day she was trafficked to Heiliang's house, for example, "almost six months ago in the evening" she carved the first mark, in the third section she is still telling "the evening of the 205th day" and "what happened on the 303rd day". But from the fourth section onwards, such accounts of marking and counting the days do not appear again. In terms of the change of ideology, we think that Hu Die's intention to escape from Geliang village became weaker. On the other hand, the more she recognizes her identity in Geliang village, the more she recognizes her identity in this village. The answer to this can be found in her own self-questioning. After the birth of her son, she once murmured to her son in his swaddling clothes: "I can't tell anyone in this village that you've come to me so what can I say. This must be fate, right? Do we deserve to be here? Why can't we be here? Didn't my mother leave the village for the city, and since she could go from the village to the city, then she could have come here too." In the face of this psychological change of Hu Die, some people may say that it is just the wishful thinking of Jia Pingwa, or more pointedly, say that it is a kind of shameful corrosion of female resistance. Either wishful thinking or ideological corrosion, the brutal reality, sympathy and discontent with the dying and decay of the rural world depicted in Jia Pingwa's writing and his stance is manifested to the fullest extent.

Is Hu Die's identity recognition real? From the point of view of the character's archetype and the internal logic of the novel, such authenticity does exist.

In the original event, the daughter of Jia Pingwa's fellow villager, after being rescued, could not bear the pressure of public opinion and left a note for her family, saying, "She has returned to that village." We can understand why she left home under the pressure of public opinion, but after leaving home, why did she go back to the village she had tried so hard to escape from? Perhaps, we can only say that she found warmth and identity there. In the novel, this identity has a solid logical foundation. First of all, Hu Die was born in the countryside and dropped out of junior high school (compare with Bai Xuemei who was a university graduate in Blind Mountain), so in terms of her upbringing and cultural level, there is not a big difference between her and Geliang village, which provides a possibility for her acceptance of Heiliang and a basis for her to find identity in Geliang village. Secondly, Heilang's family treated her very kindly, even treating her as a treasure. Although they forced her to have sex in order to keep her, they didn't regard her as a machine for reproduction or a tool for labor, and for a long time, Hei Liang respected her wishes by letting her sleep on the kang and spreading a mat under the square table for her to sleep on. Though she had vented her anger by smashing everything in the room, Heiliang did not beat her and even carried buckets of food and rice for her. Her room was lit up day and night, even though Hei Liang's family didn't bother to light the lamps because the price of oil was so expensive. Although he eats potatoes three times a day, Heilang often goes to the town to buy white steamed buns for her because he is worried that she won't be able to eat the food here, and Heilang's father tries to provide her with tasty food. Because water is very expensive, Heiliang and the others used to wash their faces one after the other, but the water they got for her was always fresh ...... All these details of her daily life were told from Hu Die's point of view, This means that she felt the kindness of the Heiliang family and the surrounding villagers to her from these little details, which brought her warmth, and these provided a solid foundation for her identity recognition in Geliang village.

The last thing that reflects the author's narrative position is the ending of the novel. Blind Mountain ends with Bai Xuemei killing Huang Degui, which is obviously a kind of tragic criticism and warning: there is no happy ending here, not Bai Xuemei being rescued, but the destruction of both sides. The movie hopes to shock with this tragedy, and to achieve the significance of critiquing reality and enlightening the public. However, Extreme Flower closes the story with a different ending. Hu Die, partly helplessly and partly consciously, gave up waiting for her mother to come to look for her. This way of ending is different from the traditional Chinese happy ending, although she gave up her efforts to leave, but from her body which gradually lost weight and turned into paper, it is not difficult to read Hu Die's pain. But it is obviously different from the elitist intellectual tragedy of Blind Mountain. It seems that Jia Pingwa may hope that Hudie can stay. The writer's soul was so close to the villagers in the northwest countryside. When he sadly cried out in the afterword "Who else pays attention to the fact that the city has taken away the wealth of the countryside, the labor of the countryside, and the women of the countryside", it is not difficult for us to imagine how much he hoped that Hu Die could stay!

For many years, deeply rooted in the rural villages of Northwest China, Jia Pingwa has been diligently writing about the rural life, sickness and death of his rural folks with his writing, as in *Qin Qiang*(The Qin Opera), *Gu Lu*(The Ancient Kilin), *Bringing the Lamp*, *Lao Sheng* (The old male role), and *Extreme Flower*.

Although the framework of *Extreme Flower* is similar to that of the movie *Blind Mountain*; However, after *Blind Mountain*, *Extreme Flower* tells a different story.

Originally published in Journal of Ankang College, Issue 6, 2016

Unconscious Divergence, Dislocation and Annihilation

-Analysis of the Naming Controversy of "New Century Literature"

According to relevant scholars, the merger of "new century" and "literature" appeared as early as 1993. However, the real concept of "New Century Literature" as a complete concept was first advocated and then widely publicized in Literary and Artistic Discourse. From the 2nd issue of 2005, when the column "About New Century Literature" was opened, to the 16th issue of 2011, in nearly seven years, Literary and Artistic Discourse has done a lot of work in advocating the study of "New Century Literature". A search on "China National Knowledge Infrastructure" using the keyword "New Century Literature" yielded the following results: as of the 16th issue of 2011, Wang Guangdong's paper "Localization of Literary Language in the New Century", a total of 72 papers were published in Literary and Artistic Discourse under the title of "New Century Literature" (the time of searching was on November 9, 2011, the same below).

Literary and Artistic Discourse's initiative has also been positively received by the academic community, with 212 articles under the title of "New Century Literature" on CNKI.

Well-known literary research journals such as the South Literary Forum (12 articles), Literary Review (7 articles), Contemporary Literary Forum (5 articles), Journal of Hainan Normal University (5 articles), Contemporary Writers' Review (3 articles), and Review of Fiction (3 articles) are also involved in varying degrees in the promotion of the research hotspot of "New Century Literature". The promotion of "New Century Literature" is also very much related to the promotion of famous scholars in the academic circles. As of November 9, 2011, searching on the CNKI, scholars who actively participated in the research of "New Century Literature" in recent years have been found to have been involved in the promotion of "New Century Literature": 6 articles by Zhang Weimin, 6 articles by Bai Ye, 6 articles by Meng Fanhua, 5 articles by Zhang Yiwu, 4 articles by Cheng Guangwei, 4 articles by Wang Chunfei, 4 articles by Wang Guangdong, 3 articles by Yu Kerxun, 3 articles by Lei Da. Moreover, since 2005, nearly 10 academic conferences have been held under the title of "New Century Literature".

Whether from the academic conferences, the number of academic papers published, or from the scholars participating in the discussions and the journals that published the papers, the study of "New Century Literature" is an indisputable hotspot in the study of contemporary Chinese literature since the new century. Some scholars have already made a preliminary sorting out and reflection on this research hotspot, such as in 2008, Bi Wenjun published "A Review of the Research on "New Century Literature" in the first issue of Southern Literature Forum, and in 2011, Luo Changqing published "An Overview of the Critical Phenomenon of "New Century Literature" in the third issue of Jinyang Academic Journal. In 2011, Luo Changqing published "An Overview of the Critical Phenomenon of New Century Literature" in the third issue of Jinyang Academic Journal. Although Bi Wenjun's article is titled "Review", the issues she discusses are obviously focused on the reflection on the criticism of "New Century Literature", and the contents of the reflection include: the relationship between literature and history, the boundaries between the study of literary history and the criticism, the perspectives and vision of literature study, and the mentality and position of the researcher etc. Luo Changqing's article focuses more on sorting out the development of "New Century Literature" criticism, such as the reasons for the rise of "New Century Literature" criticism, some examples of why it has become a hot topic of research, and the consensus and differences in criticism, etc.

Unlike the two articles mentioned above, this paper focuses on the academic divisions within the camp of scholars constructing "New Century Literature" during the naming dispute over "New Century Literature," as well as the 'misalignment' phenomenon that emerged when the academic community criticized the naming of New Century New Century Literature and the 'misalignment' phenomenon that emerged when the academic community criticized the naming of"New Century Literature." Through this analysis, it seeks to reveal the potential chaos in academic research within the current academic environment, which is pulled in multiple directions and surrounded by various forces, as well as the potential obfuscation of genuine academic research in this chaos.

The concept of "New Century Literature" as a concept of literary criticism (some scholars even want to construct it as a concept of literary history) was basically advocated by the Literary and Artistic Discourse, and scholars who support this concept basically state their viewpoints in this journal. In addition to Zhang Weimin, the former editor-in-chief of Literary and Artistic Discourse, famous scholars who support this concept include Lei Da, Bai Ye, Yu Kexun, Zhang Yiwu, etc. Especially Lei Da, who has made the most effort in the conceptualization and construction of the history of "New Century Literature" and the history of literature, and has made the most obvious academic contributions.

I. Internal Disagreements among the Constructors of "New Century Literature"

From existing literature, we cannot definitively determine whether Lei Da and Zhang Weimin were fully aware of their academic differences.

However, based on Lei Da's choice of platform for publishing his research paper on "New Century Literature" [1] and Zhang Weimin's actual

1 Lei Da's five essays on "New Century Literature", "A Preliminary Discussion on New Century Literature: The Orientation of Chinese Literature in the New Century", "New

actions in editing the selected papers for New Century Literature Studies[1], we cannot discern any clear recognition of the academic differences between the two. The lack of awareness or reluctance to publicize the differences does not mean that they did not exist. The fact that they did not realize it or did not want to publicize it does not mean that the disagreement did not exist. Through careful reading of Lei Da and Zhang Weimin's research papers on "New Century Literature", we found that there are great differences between them in advocating and defining the concept of "New Century Literature" and summarizing the characteristics of "New Century Literature".

(i) Differences in Advocating the Concept of New Century Literature

The concept of "New Century Literature" was jointly advocated and promoted by Zhang Weimin, Bai Ye, Lei Da, and Zhang Yiwu. Through the joint advocacy and promotion of these famous scholars or editors-in-chief of famous critical magazines, the concept of "New Century Literature" soon exerted a great impact in the contemporary literary and critical circles. However, behind this academic hotspot, which appeared to be quite lively at first sight, there lurked a real academic embarrassment, which had lurked since the concept was first advocated.

Scholars such as Lei Da and Zhang Yiwu, who advocated "New Century Literature," felt that China's cultural environment underwent significant changes in the 1990s, particularly after Deng Xiaoping's Southern Talks in

---

Century Literature: Conceptual Generation, Connectedness and Aesthetic Characteristics", "An Overview of Long Fiction since the New Century", "New Century Literature: Why I advocate the term "New Century Literature"" and "The Orientation of Chinese Literature in the New Century Decade", are all in one place. An Overview of Long Novels since the New Century", "New Century Literature - Why I advocate the term "New Century Literature" and "The Trend of Chinese Literature in the New Century Decade", all of which were published in Literary Controversy.

1 Zhang Weimin, Meng Chunrui, Zhu Xuanxiang, editors: New Century Literature Research, People's Literature Publishing House, 2007. In this anthology of essays, many of Radar's essays on the study of "New Century Literature" are included.

1992. They even argued that "a new cultural form of the 'New Century' had already begun to take shape." [1]This change may lead (and seems to have already led) to some new features in Chinese literature. This change may lead (and seems to have led to) some new characteristics of Chinese literature, which are distinctly different from the "New Period Literature. In order to show this difference, they feel that it is necessary to propose a new concept of literary history to summarize the literature of this period. This was the first reason why Lei Da and others proposed the concept of "New Century Literature". It should be said that their senses are still quite sensitive, and there is a quite obvious difference between contemporary literature since the 1990s and "New Century Literature", especially the literature before the 1980s.

The second reason why Lei Da and others put forward the concept of "New Century Literature" is the dissatisfaction with the phasing of the history of modern and contemporary Chinese literature. According to Lei Da, the concept of "New Period Literature" has been called "New Period Literature" for almost thirty years, a length of time close to that of modern literature, and the current Chinese literature is very different from what it was when it was first named "New Period Literature", so it is inappropriate to continue to use this concept, and it seems to be the wish of all to replace it with a new one".[2]

The third reason is that in the 1990s, concepts such as "post-new period" were proposed by Xie Mian, Lei Da, Zhang Yiwu, and Rao Pengzi provided literary historical theoretical resources for the introduction of the concept of "new century literature." They believed that as early as that time, people had already recognized the trend toward literary transformation, and that " Fu

---

1 Zhang Yiwu, "New Century Literature: Reflections on Crossing Out of New Literature", Literary and Artistic Discourse, No. 4, 2005.
2 Lei Da: "On New Century Literature" - Why I Advocate the Proposal of New Century Literature", Literary and Artistic Discourse, No. 2, 2007.

Xiuyan explored the prospects of literary narrative, Kong Fanjin from the realistic spirit of literature, Sun Zhongtian from the transformation of discourse concepts to literary structures, Zhao Xueyong from the local nature of literature, and Li Yi from the intrinsic connection between the nationality and modernity of literature, collectively envisioned the utopia of 'New Century Literature,' thereby making the concept of 'New Century Literature' widely accepted."[1]

The last reason should be Zhang Weimin's column "On New Century Literature" in the second issue of Literary Controversy in 2005. In this academic column, Zhang Weimin wrote a lengthy "Editor's Note", which demonstrated his ambition to advocate the study of "New Century Literature". In this article, titled "New Manifestations in the New Century: Editor's Words on the Opening Column", Zhang Weimin put forward his reasons for opening a column on "Literature of the New Century" and advocating the study of "New Century Literature". He thinks that "since literature has been developed for a period of time since the new century, can we find out some new features and manifestations of it in this period of accumulation? In a word, the basic theme of our discussion is to see what new manifestations of the literature of the new century there are, which naturally includes the judgment and opinion on the literature of the new century "[2]. From this passage, we can see that Zhang Weimin's research on "New Century Literature" is mainly to summarize the literary development since the new century, which is somewhat reminiscent of the tone of government work reports summarizing recent achievements.

---

1 Lei Da and Ren Donghua, "New Century Literature: Conceptualization, Relevance and Aesthetic Characteristics", Literary and Artistic Discourse, No.4, 2006.
2 Zhang Weimin, "New Century, New Expression: Editor's Words on the Opening Column", Literary and Artistic Discourse, No. 2, 2005.

From the above summary of the reasons why scholars advocate the study of "New Age Literature", Zhang Weimin and Reda's understanding of "New Century Literature" is in fact very different. Basically from the point of view of literary history, Lei Da firstly found out that in the process of literary development since 1990, some characteristics different from those of the "New Period Literature" had appeared, which could no longer be summarized by the concept of "New Period Literature", therefore, he attempted to use theoretical resources from previous literary history to divide this period of literature into stages. In other words, Lei Da firstly discovered the "new quality" in the process of literary development, and then looked at this literary history with a historian's eye on the "new quality". Unlike Lei Da, Zhang Weimin's approach to the study of "New Century Literature" is basically critical. He is not sure whether the literature since the New Century has a "new quality" or not. [1]He only feels that a period of time has passed since the New Century. He only felt that the "New Century" had already passed for some time, and that we should make a timely summary of the literary development during this period, and he did not care much whether the result was a "new performance" or an "old" one, for he did not make any reference to the history of literature here. He did not have the slightest intention of staging the history of literature.

If there is such a big difference in the understanding of "New Century Literature" between the two sides, why are they still on the same side in this heated naming dispute?

---

1 For example, in his article "New Century, New Expression: The Editor's Preface," he explicitly states: "New Century' literature does not necessarily have to have any 'new expression'; what it expresses may still be 'old' expression. However, even if this is the case, we must still point out in our discussions that it represents a new round of growth within the continuity of tradition. Moreover, whether Chinese literature since the New Century has any 'new expression' or what forms such 'new expression' may take will ultimately be determined through future discussions."

Perhaps we can only understand it as follows: we all get what we want. For Lei Da, it was a platform to focus on his academic ideas, while for Zhang Weimin, it was the support of a renowned scholar in the academic world. It is impossible to know whether Lei Da was aware of this great difference between them when he and Zhang Weimin "collaborated", but the academic embarrassment had already begun from the very beginning of their "collaboration".

(ii) Differences in defining the concept of "New Century Literature

What, then, is "New Century Literature"?

Some scholars have avoided a conceptualization of "New Century Literature". We believe that this is partly because they have realized that this concept is prone to criticism, and perhaps more importantly, because they themselves are still in a state of wait-and-see with regard to "New Century Literature". This also seems to indicate the fragility of the concept of "New Century Literature" in another way.

Among the scholars who have tried to conceptualize "New Century Literature", Lei Da's concept should be relatively easy to accept. However, comparing the articles published by Lei Da, we find that he himself seems to have some contradictions and confusions. In his article "New Century Literature - The Direction of Chinese Literature since the New Century", he argues that taking the year 2000 as the "symbolic starting point" of the "New Century Literature", although "on the one hand, it turns 'New Century Literature' from a casual capture of time into a conscious interruption of literary development, obscuring the tradition and commonality of 'New Century Literature'; on the other hand, it suspends the new quality of literature on which its name is based. " However, "We are currently unable to propose a more reasonable or necessary concept than 'New Century Literature."[1] It is obvious that he takes 2000 as the "symbolic beginning" of the "New Century Literature". However, in the article "The Birth of the Concept of New Century Literature, its Connectedness and Aesthetic Characteristics", he proposes to "let the 'New Century Literature' refer to the literature since the 1990s". He also said that "if we take 1992 as the starting point, then 'New Century Literature' has been in development for more than ten years". In his "On 'New Century Literature' - Why I Advocate the Formulation of 'New Century Literature'", he advocates that the 1990s should be regarded as the preparatory period of "New Century Literature", while "New Century Literature" should be used to refer to "Literature of the post-2000 period up to the present day", or "Literature of the 21st Century and beyond". In his article "The Trend of Chinese Literature in the Decade of the New Century", Lei Da seems to have reinforced his idea of "preparatory period". He reminds us, "there is a preparatory or transitional period for 'New Century Literature', roughly referring to the seven or eight years from 1993. It would be unscientific not to see this preparatory period. However, according to the conventional expression, it must be counted from the year 2000."[2] Let's take a look at the time of publication of these articles, namely, the 3rd issue of 2005, the 4th issue of 2006, the 2nd issue of 2007, and the 2nd issue of 2010 of Literary and Artistic Discourse. That is to say, although after 2007 Radar basically insisted on 2000 as the opening year of the "New Century Literature", and the 1990s as its preparatory period, however, he had a period of hesitation, he tried to use the term "New Century Literature" to refer to the literature since the 1990s, probably because he felt that the period of the 1990s did not

1 Lei Da and Ren Donghua, "New Century Literature: A Preliminary Discussion on the Direction of Chinese Literature since the New Century", Literature and Art Controversy, No. 3, 2005.

2 Lei Da, Ren Donghua: The Trend of Chinese Literature in the New Century), Literary Arts Controversy, No. 2, 2010.

fit well with the name of the "New Century", and then he considered it as the preparatory period of the "New Century Literature". We should not underestimate this "hesitation", which is exactly a point of theoretical difference between Lei Da and Bai Ye and Zhang Weimin, and also an opportunity for Lei Da to strike back at his opponents. Unfortunately, however, Lei Da has categorized the literature of the 90s as "preparatory" for fear that the name does not match the reality, and this precisely gives reason to those who criticize him. According to our analysis, Lei Da could have referred to the practice of "Twentieth Century Chinese Literature" and categorized the literature of the 1990s into "New Century Literature" (of course, whether this name is appropriate or not is another story), in which case his theory of literary history might be more mature.

For Lei Da, "New Century Literature" is mainly a relative historical concept of literature. He tries to use this concept to make contemporary literary research say goodbye to "New Period Literature". Therefore, he thinks that "in essence, the concept of 'New Century Literature' still belongs to the disciplinary category of 'Contemporary Literature', only that its concept has a distinctly relative nature, and most people use it mainly in relation to 'New Period Literature'." Moreover, "it is not a purely temporal concept, what it emphasizes is mainly the changes in the process of literary development rather than time ". [1]Therefore, to Lei Da, "New Century Literature" is not only a confusing and expedient choice, but also, an idea that is easier to understand by the academic circles.

Compared to Lei Da, Zhang Weimin's understanding of "New Century Literature" is almost entirely a different picture. In terms of the concept of "New Century Literature", Zhang Weimin's logical starting point is basically

---

1 Lei Da: On "New Century Literature" - Why I Advocate the Proposal of "New Century Literature", Literary and Artistic Discourse, No.2, 2007.

the "new century" and "new phenomenon", and the purpose of his research on "New Century Literature" is mainly to summarize the literary achievements since the new century. When advocating the study of "New Century Literature", Zhang Weimin said, "We are living in a new century. As a matter of fact, as far as Chinese literary criticism is concerned, the object of its attention and tracking is none other than the 'literature of the new century'."[1] From this we can see that for Zhang Weimin, the study of "New Century Literature" should be more accurately described as a kind of literary criticism; however, for Lei Da, it is more of a delineation and interpretation of literary history. There is a big difference in their thinking. We can even say that Zhang's "New Century Literature" is not Lei's "New Century Literature". In Zhang Weimin's case, "New Century" is mainly a temporal concept, but for Lei Da, "New Century" is more in the nature of literary history.

Therefore, their considerations on the starting point of "new century literature" are also very different. Though Lei Da, based on various considerations, set the starting point of "new century literature" at 2000, the literature of the 90's has never been out of his field of investigation, and he is more concerned with the consistency of the nature of literature. However, for Zhang Weimin, the literature of the 1990s is not only out of his field of investigation, but has even become the antithesis of the "New Century Literature" which Zhang Weimin is trying to surpass. When Zhang Weimin advocated the study of "New Century Literature", he pointed out that "'New Century Literature has a much broader and more attractive scope than the concepts of 'New Period Literature' and 'Literature of the 90s' and 'Literature of the 80s' in the last century, there is a broader and more attractive space for expression and exploration, which is not only the closest to us, but also has a future; it is not only an objective object of cognition, but also a developing

1 Zhang Weimin, "Conducting Research on 'New Century Literature'", Literature and Art Controversy, No. 1, 2006.

and changing object of cognition".[1] Although Bai Ye's argument is not like Zhang Weimin's, who tries to simply sweep literature of the 90's into the dark corner of history, it is also not like Lei Da's, who emphasizes the homogeneity between literature of the 90's and the "new century literature". Unlike Lei Da, who emphasized the historical connection between the literature of the 90s and the "New Century Literature", Bai Ye emphasized the "break" between the two. He thinks that "after entering the new century, literature has continued to mutate in the profound transformation from the outside to the inside that had already taken place in the 1990s; five years later, although it is far from being finalized, it can be seen that although there are still some inheritance and linkage between the literature of the new century and the 80s and 90s, they have become more and more different.". [2]When Zhang Weimin and Bai Ye put the literature of the 90's in opposition to the "New Century Literature", it is unavoidable to invite criticisms, because a clear fact of literary history tells us that the literature of the 90's and the so-called "New Century Literature" do not have much difference; on the contrary, their similarities are easier to spot.

(iii) The difference in the characteristics: new century literature and other periods.

In the long history of literary development, in addition to giving the reasons for the staging of history and defining a new historical period, there is one more thing that must be done in order to distinguish a certain period of literary history and rename it independently, that is, to summarize the new characteristics of literature in this new historical period. It is only with the new features that the literature of this period may have the most solid

1 Zhang Weimin, "Conducting Research on 'New Century Literature'", Literary Arts Controversy, No. 1, 2006.
2 Bai Ye, "The New Format and New Subjects of Literature in the New Century", Literary and Artistic Controversy, No. 4, 2006.

foundation for becoming a new historical period. Otherwise, why should we isolate it from history?

The advocates of "New Century Literature" naturally understand this rationale. In the relevant articles of Lei Da and Zhang Weimin, we also read their summarization of the characteristics of "New Century Literature". If the starting point of the question is the same, their summarization of the characteristics of "new century literature" should be similar, or at least within the same discourse system. Unfortunately, however, this is not the case.

In the article "A Preliminary Discussion on New Century Literature - The Orientation of Chinese Literature since the New Century", Lei Da summarizes the characteristics of "New Century Literature" in the following aspects: 1. The influence of the market economy. The market economy has changed the original mode of production and operation of literature (from ideological creation to commercialized production); the market economy has changed the main target of literary creation (from rural to urban); the market economy has profoundly affected the change of the function of literature (from educational function to consumption function). 2. Globalized cultural contexts. The globalized context has given a strong impetus and wide spiritual influence to the "New Century Literature". Writers began to focus on "Orientality", "Chineseness" and "Ethnicity" from a globalized perspective. 3. The profound influence of science. The expansion of scientific thinking in literary creation has become an obvious trend in the literature of the new century. Moreover, the development of science and technology has also catalyzed a "third kind of literature in human civilization": multimedia literature. 4. The promotion of political civilization and the return to a political perspective. 5. Literature opens up new horizons of daily aesthetics. 6. Literature explores the depth of human nature under a multi-dimensional perspective.

In "New Century Literature: Conceptual Formation, Relevance and Aesthetic Characteristics", Lei Da summarized the characteristics of "New

Century Literature" as follows: the formation of "literary metropolis"; the main melody of "national soul re-casting" and its variations; the diversification of literary values; the transformation of imagination ("political imagination" into "the common imagination of the people"); new aesthetic forms (including linguistic order, expressive techniques and stylistic rheology).

When we combine the characteristics summarized in Lei Da's two articles, we find that Lei Da's main concerns are mainly: the spiritual world of writers (global, national, scientific thinking), the way of literary creation, the target audience of literary expression, the function of literature, the theme of literary expression (politics, daily life, human nature), the value orientation of literature, and the forms of literary expression, etc.

We then look at the main characteristics of "New Age literature" summarized by Zhang Weimin. His reflections on this issue are mainly reflected in "Some Points on the Characteristics of New Age Literature". He thinks that the main features of the "literature of the new century" include the following aspects: the literature of increment, the literature of growth, the literature of totality, the literature of life, the literature of physical objects and the literature of "civilization". Let's not say that such terms have much rationality (it is really not easy to sort out the specific connotation of these terms), we only have to ask: can these characteristics be called the "new" proof of "new century literature"? The answer, I am afraid, is a bit disappointing - aren't all these "characteristics" fully justifiable to summarize the literature of any era? What's more, what's more crucial is that his words are basically not in the same system as Lei Da's. When Lei Da summarized the characteristics of "New Century Literature", he basically developed it within the more traditional discourse system of Marxist literary theory. But to what system does Zhang Weimin's discourse belong? We cannot say. But there is one thing we can be sure of, the starting point of his thinking on this issue is different from that of Lei Da.

Through the analysis of the characteristics of "New Century Literature" summarized by Lei Da and Zhang Weimin, we find that not only are the characteristics summarized by the two men very different, but also the two have different starting points and different discourse systems when they think about this issue. This once again proves our point: the "new century literature" they study is basically not the same thing.

II. The dislocation of criticism and the annihilation of academics

The coinage of "New Century Literature" was met with much criticism as soon as it was put forward.

The reasons for the criticism can be summarized as follows.

The first reason, and the one that has been put forward most often, is the relationship between "New Century Literature" and the literature of the 1990s. The opponents think that the relationship between the two is not "broken" as Zhang Weimin and Bai Ye said, but more of a kind of consistency. Hui Yan Bing's critical article "The Fate of the Strong and the Powerless Resistance - Reflection on the Naming of "New Century Literature" is perhaps the most intense and influential of all the critical articles. He thinks that "in terms of the literary practice in the past five years (i.e. from 2000 to 2005 - citation needed), compared with the literature of the 1990s, the dimensions of literary aesthetics have not changed, the ways in which meaning is generated have not changed, and the artistic quality of the texts have not changed. Even the most basic external supports, such as social transformation, historical rewriting, and ideological reset, are lacking. Yet, people are awkwardly dissecting the literary chain and forcibly explaining the differences, which is truly baffling". Since there is no quality that can produce a "break" between "New Century Literature" and the literature of the 1990s, there is no reason for "New Century Literature" to become an independent phase of literary history. The concept of "New Century Literature" is also a concept that cannot be established. So, what are the reasons for advocating this concept? According to Hui Yanbing, "the naming of 'new century literature' is only a repetition of the contemporary tradition of literary history (the reliance on the notion of time - cited)." "Behind the naming of 'New Century Literature' is the emptiness of contemporary literary research and literary criticism".[1] The second reason is put forward by Wu Sijing. Wu Sijing thinks that it is necessary to name the literature since the new century to distinguish it from the "New Period Literature" which has a strong political meaning, but at the beginning of the 21st century, naming the literature of the past ten years with the time span of a century does not match with the name, so he suggests to use the term "early 21st century literature". [2]What Wu Sijing pointed out is in fact a common-sense problem in naming literary history: literary history is usually named after a certain period of literary history has passed, and literary historians summarize this period of literary history and then name it according to its literary style or literary history characteristics. Now that the new century has just begun, it is obviously inappropriate to hasten to use the time span of a century to name a literature that has only been in existence for ten years. However, this naming behavior of Lei Da and others is not original. Since the emergence of the concept of "contemporary literature", this kind of naming impulse to anticipate the future development of literature has appeared again and again. Isn't "Contemporary Literature", "New Period Literature" and even "Post-New Age Literature" the result of this impulse to "presuppose" the future?

The third reason for opposition was that "New Century Literature" lacked literary achievements to support its independent existence. According

---

1 Hui Yanbing, "Strong Fate and Powerless Resistance: Reflections on the Naming of "New Century Literature", Literary Review, No. 5, 2006.

2 Wu Sijing: "New Century Literature", or "Literature at the Beginning of the Century"? - Reflections on the Naming of Literature Nowadays", Wen Yi Zheng Ming, No. 2, 2007.

to Liu Weidong, "New Century Literature lacks the achievements of new literature and the self-confidence of the participants in the achievements". "The discussion of the new century literature should be based on the understanding of the new century literary works. However, in the critics' discourse, some important elements of the new century that are irrelevant to literary works have been taken for granted,while literature has been placed in a subordinate position to these elements. [1]

It has also been argued that the designation "New Century Literature" is in fact a new reaction to the theory of literary evolution, and like the concept of 'New Period Literature', it cannot be self-attested. Literary 'rupture' has its roots in the need for evolution of literary concepts, and is therefore more often than not a fictional mode of discourse, 'invented' by critics as a strategy of literary narrative."[2]

Summarizing the reasons of the scholars' criticisms, we find that when they criticized the concept, they simply did not realize the great difference between the concepts of Lei Da and Zhang Weimin's "New Century Literature". In spite of this, they all criticized Lei Da and Zhang Weimin together. From the content of their criticism, they mainly criticized Zhang Weimin's viewpoints, and if they expanded a little, they could have included Bai Ye, but Lei Da should not have been in the seat of their criticism, because the reasons for their criticisms could not be established. According to Lei Da's understanding of "New Century Literature", apart from the fact that the term "New Century Literature" is not very appropriate, the following are some of the reasons for Lei Da's criticisms: by including 1990s literature in the scope of "New Century Literature", emphasizing the consistency between the two

---

1 Liu Weidong, "New Century Literature in the Critical Discourse of the New Century - Taking the Construction of New Century Literature by Literary Controversy as an Example", Novel Review, No. 1, 2006.
2 Long Yangzhi: "Fracture: A Critique of the Legitimacy of New Century Literature", Art Wide Angle, No.3, 2008.

can only serve as a reason to support "New Century Literature," but it cannot be used as a reason to oppose the study of "New Century Literature."

Looking at literature from the 1990s to the present, the literary achievement is no longer an issue. Since Lei Da emphasizes the changing aspect of "New Century Literature" in relation to "New Period Literature", the accusation of "Literary Evolution Theory" seems to be difficult to resonate with. However, as we have analyzed earlier, on the one hand, the critics' "one-pot" strategy of criticism confuses the difference between Lei Da and Zhang Weimin, and the heated criticism obliterates Lei Da's academic thinking. [1] On the other hand, people's criticism of Lei Da is not totally unjustified, because he has his own contradictions in the temporal limitation of the concept and the 1990s have been an unresolved problem in his concept of "New Century Literature". In our opinion, from Lei Da's initial understanding, the literature of the 1990s should be a part of the "New Century Literature", but in order to expand his own academic camp, to win a centralized position for his publications, and thus to expand his academic influence, he changed his academic judgment which should not have been changed, and as a result, together with Zhang Weimin, he was put in a position to be criticized.

In 2011, Literary and Artistic Discourse changed its editor-in-chief, with Zhang Weimin and Zhu Jing retiring, and the new editor-in-chief, Wang Shuanglong, making an important shift in his thinking about running the journal, no longer keen on "making up neologisms to attract attention", it is more concerned with the discovery and analysis of literary issues. In this way, the

---

1 ① So, in his article "Why is it always difficult to find a true and thorough critical voice" published in Contemporary Writers' Review, Issue 2, 2011, Reda sighed helplessly: "In China, there is seldom a time when literary criticism was as weak and passive as it is today, embarrassed and helpless, unable to find its own irreplaceable and independent position amidst the pulls and siege of multiple forces. It is also difficult to find a way to get out of the predicament and move forward." In our opinion, this kind of feeling comes more from his own experience.

study of "New Century Literature", which is mainly initiated by "Literary and Artistic Discourse" and gradually attracted the attention of scholars, without a centralized academic position, will end up as a cloud in history.

If the study of "New Century Literature" is only an academic "hot spot" "created" by a certain academic publication, there is nothing to regret its withdrawal from the stage of history. However, judging from the studies of "New Century Literature" by scholars such as Lei Da, it seems that this is not the case. There is a real academic thinking here. In this case, what has gone with the wind is not only a cultural bubble under the banner of academia, but also academic thinking that might have made some progress in the depths of history. However, it is regrettable that, the critical community did not seriously analyze the huge differences within the advocates of the "new century literature". With the tide of this rapid exit from the historical stage, Lei Da's academic thinking that might have made some contribution to the construction of the history of contemporary literature has gradually declined and finally disappeared in an academic environment where many forces are pulling and blocking it. This is the first layer of what we mean by "academic annihilation".

By this we also mean Lei Da's personal thinking (or rather, strategy). Although it is more reasonable to consider the 1990s as a period of preparation for the "new century literature" rather than simply as an object to be surpassed by the "new century literature," the "preparation period" does not belong to the real "new century literature" in terms of logical relations, after all.

It seems that the real "New Century Literature" has more historical legitimacy than the literature of the 1990s and belongs to a higher level of literary stage. Behind this kind of thinking (strategy) is still the "literary evolution" that the critics are pointing at. Moreover, from the actual situation of literature, we really cannot see any real and essential difference between the so-called "new century literature" of and the literature of the 1990s. If that is the case, why don't we categorize the literature of the 1990s and the "new century literature" into one historical stage? The crux of the problem lies in the name of "New Century Literature". The 1990s is obviously the end of the 20th century, if it is categorized into "New Century Literature", it is not in the right name. At this time, should we respect the historical facts of literature and change the name, or should we cut the footsteps to fit the so-called "New Century Literature" concept for the sake of the "rightful name"? If it is really for the sake of academic research, the answer is self-evident. But why did Lei Da choose the latter?

Naturally, it is the present-day academic environment that influences him to change his narrative strategy. We are in a cultural environment where many forces are pulling and blocking us. This is an era of information explosion and information overload. How will the audience choose in the face of the tidal wave of information coming at them? This is a question that every information transmitter has to consider seriously. Specifically, this is also true for academic research: we have numerous academic journals, publish countless academic papers and monographs each year, but how many people actually read these papers and monographs? How do readers know which papers and monographs have real academic value? Under such a situation, it is not easy to make one's voice heard in the academic world, especially the voice that one thinks should attract attention.

This is where the power of the media comes into play. If there is an academic journal that can provide itself with a stage to express its own academic ideas and focus on publishing its own research articles in this field, we think that at this time, most scholars won't be too concerned about the relationship between the "name" and the "reality". We can understand the helplessness of the scholars, but the real academics may be annihilated and disappear in this kind of compromise and helplessness. Does this also show the sadness of current academic research to a certain extent?

A Long Way to Go

- Analysis of Disciplinarization of Cyber Literature Research in the New Century

If we count from 1998, when Pizi Cai, an online writer from Taiwan, China, published The First Intimate Contact and became popular in mainland China, it has been more than a decade since the development of Cyber literature in mainland China. In the past decade or so, cyber literature has quietly emerged as a noteworthy scene in the contemporary literary scene since the new century. Literary websites, the homepage of Personal Literature, the literary channels of web portals, electronic literary journals, blogs, and various kinds of hypertext literary experiments have become the hot topics among readers, especially the young generation of readers. In the face of such a booming and bustling situation of online literature, the academic world has also made positive responses. A search on the CNKI reveals that so far (as of October 8, 2012, the same below), a total of 913 papers with the title of "cyberliterature", 2,137 papers with the theme of "cyberliterature", 251 master's theses and 16 doctoral dissertations have been published by academics. Important Issues in the Field of Contemporary Literature and Literary Theory have also been involved in the discussion of cyber literature to different degrees. As of October 8, 2012, the Journal of South-Central University published 18 articles on the topic of network literature, 15 articles in Contemporary Literature Forum, 15 articles in Southern Literature Forum and Literary Controversy, and 8 articles in Literary Review and Literary Theory and Criticism. Research works related to Cyber literature have also been published, such as Ouyang Youquan's "Outline of Cyber Literature", "Ontology of Cyber Literature", "Theological Formation of Cyber Literature", "History of Cyber Literature - A Survey of Chinese Cyber Literature", etc. At the beginning of the new century, cyber literature has also entered the university classroom and has its own teaching materials, such as Introduction to

Cyberliterature edited by Ouyang Youquan of Central South University, Cyberliterature edited by Mei Hong of Xi'an Jiaotong University, etc. Needless to say, "Cyber literature" has become an unavoidable hot spot in the study of Chinese contemporary literature since the new century. Moreover, a considerable number of scholars hope to realize the disciplining of the study of Cyber literature through their own efforts. What is the situation of this seemingly prosperous academic research? Has the effort of disciplinarization been realized? In this paper, we will sort out the research on Cyber literature since the new century in terms of the concept of Cyber literature, the development of Cyber literature, the characteristics of Cyber literature, the relationship between Cyber literature and traditional literature, the development trend of Cyber literature, and the problems of Cyber literature, etc., and hope to reflect on the current research on Cyber literature through this sorting out, so as to make our humble efforts to realize the disciplinarization of the research on Cyber literature.

To be or not to be, that is the question - The existence and concept of cyber literature

In our thinking habit, in order to study a certain object, we must first find out whether there is such a thing. If it does exist, can we grasp it in the form of an abstract concept? If something does not exist, why should we waste our time studying it? To do so, we must have a definition: what is this thing? Only then can we know how to proceed. However, in the field of literary theory, the existence of "literature" and its concepts have always been the subject of much debate among literary theorists, which has never been resolved. The same applies to Cyber literature.

One of the first questions that scholars face is: Is there a cyber literature? If there is, how to define it? This seemingly basic question has always been troubling every scholar in the study of Cyber literature. Because the existence and definition of literature is itself a very difficult problem to solve, and now with the entangled relationship between cyber literature and traditional literature, the difficulty of defining cyber literature can be imagined. Although more than ten years have passed, it seems that the problem has not been fundamentally solved.

Some scholars simply deny the existence of cyber literature. According to Li Jingze, "Literature arises from the mind, not from cyberspace, and the special problem we are facing now is that the network has been taken as the content and form of the mind in a kind of shocking ego-induced hallucination, and that is why there is that 'Cyber literature'".[1]

Li Jiefei "strongly recommended that the term 'literature' be left aside to talk about online writing. Internet writing was not created for the purpose of 'literature' at all".[2]Pizi Cai, known for his cyber literature, is also cautious about the concept of "cyber literature". He said, "If anything published on the Internet is considered a network novel, then what if Cao Xueqin comes back to life and puts Dream of Red Mansions on the Internet? Is Dream of Red Mansions a network novel?" [3] He thinks, cyber literature is still in the beginning stage, many situations are still not very clear, and it is not yet time to define cyber literature. Only after the cyber literature is more diversified, can we select the excellent works from it, summarize and conclude, and then we can give a more accurate definition of cyber literature.

But more people think that the creation and development of cyber literature is already an indisputable fact in contemporary Chinese literature. The College of Arts and Letters of China Central South University should be regarded as the major town of cyber literature research in China, and its leader, Ouyang Youquan, has published a lot of academic papers and works on cyber

---

1 Li Jingze, "Network Literature: Points and Doubts", Prose Selection, No. 9, 2000.
2 Li Jiefei: "Free and Network Writing", Prose Selection, No. 9, 2000.
3 Cai Zhiheng: Network Literature and Me, cited in Ouyang Youquan, Introduction to Network Literature, Peking University Press, 2008, p. 2.

literature research. In Ouyang Youquan's doctoral thesis, "Research on the Ontology of Cyber Literature", he is clearly affirmative of cyber literature. According to Ouyang Youquan, there are both explicit and implicit dimensions in the ontology of cyber literature, with the explicit dimension presenting a hierarchical transformation of "the art of literature - the imitation of art - the imitation of life", while the implicit values are: the transformation of literary institutions, folklore, e-poetry, cultural representations, and humanistic connotations.

According to some scholars, cyber literature is a new type of literary style created by computers, uploaded and broadcasted on the Internet for Internet users to browse or participate. It has three common types: Firstly, the works disseminated on the Internet after the electronic dissemination of traditional paper-mediated printed texts, which is cyber literature in a broad sense, and the difference between it and traditional literature is only reflected in the difference in the medium of dissemination; secondly, the original textual works created by computers and first published on the Internet, which are not only different from traditional literature in terms of carriers but also different from the original works of the netizens and the network's first publication; and the third category is hypertext and multimedia works (such as novels and multimedia scripts) created by using computer multimedia technology and Internet interaction, as well as "machine works" automatically generated with the help of specific computer software, which cannot survive without the Internet, and thus this is cyber literature in a narrower sense and cyberliterature in the real sense.[1]Since then, these three forms of cyber literature have been referred to as Internet literature, online literature and "hypertext" literature.

---

1 Ouyang Youquan, "An Outline of the Ontology of Network Literature", Literary Review, No. 6, 2004.

In the face of the difficulty of defining cyber literature theoretically, some scholars think that the theoretical definition of cyber literature can be bypassed on the premise of recognizing the existence of cyber literature, and the fact of cyber literature can be described from the perspective of application. In fact, this approach should be borrowed from the traditional field of literary theory. Some scholars advocate bypassing the definition of "literature" and going directly into the study of various aspects of literature. Specifically, Zhu Weilian, editor-in-chief of an original literary website, believes that "network literature is the popular literature of the new era; the infinite extension of the Internet has created fertile ground, and the popularization of free creative space has made the world even more expansive. Without the hassle of printing and paper, without the restrictions imposed by publishers and booksellers, countless people have taken up the pen, and an article originating from the hands of an ordinary person can instantly reach thousands of households"[1]. This is not so much a definition as a strategy. Its theoretical basis is also obvious. At a time when the characteristics of Internet literature have not been fully expressed or effectively summarized, instead of forcing a definition of Internet literature, we should choose a more appropriate way to accurately describe the state of Cyber literature. The obvious reason is that the naming of an object is often realized through the historical choice of convention rather than the attempt at coercion.

Twenty Years of Stormy Road - The Development of Internet Literature

Nowadays, the research paradigm of Internet literature in academia is mainly academic criticism. This is actually quite normal. After all, Internet literature has just developed for twenty-one years. In the academic world, it is generally regarded as contemporary literature, a part of the new century literature. Literary criticism is a major way of researching such new literature.

1 Zhu Weilian, "Fertile Soil for Literary Development," Literary Journal, February 17, 2000.

However, there are still some scholars who have paid attention to the history of the development of Cyber literature. So, what is the history of Cyber literature in the past twenty-one years?

Regarding the birth of Chinese cyber literature and its budding overseas, Ouyang Youquan, has done a preliminary sorting out. According to his research, the world's first Chinese electronic weekly, Huaxia Digest, was born on April 5, 1991, in the United States. In the same year, Wang Xiaofei founded the Overseas Chinese Poetry Newsletter, a website that is considered to be the first germ of Chinese online literature. The first original work of Chinese online literature that can be found so far is the miscellaneous article "Unwilling to be a Child Emperor" published in the 3rd issue of Huaxia Digest on April 16, 1991, signed by Zhang Langlang. The first original novel in Chinese online literature was Rat Civilization, published in Huaxia Digest, No.31, November 1, 1991, by an anonymous author. In 1994, Fang Zhouzi and others founded the first Chinese online literature publication, New Words. In 1995, Shiyang and Lu Ming founded the Chinese online poetry magazine Olive Tree, and in 1996, the first Chinese online women's literature publication, Tricks, was launched.

In 1994, the Internet landed on the Chinese mainland. In 1997, Banyan Tree, the largest Chinese original literature website in China, was established in Shanghai.[1] Since then, Cyber literature has taken root on the mainland and rapidly grown into a force to be reckoned with in the contemporary Chinese literary scene.

Naturally, scholars' research is not limited to an intellectual archaeology of the development of Internet literature. Many scholars have already begun to position the Chinese Internet literature of the past twenty years in stages.

---

1 Ouyang Youquan, "Digital Media and the Transformation of Chinese Literature," China Social Science, No. 1, 2007.

Ouyang Youquan summarizes the development of mainland Internet literature as "three impulses".

The emergence of the "five black horses" (Xing Yusen, Ning Caishen, Yu Baimei, Li Xunhuan and Anne Baby) in Mainland China's cyber literature has been regarded as the first wave of cyber literature. The "Best Cyber Literature" of 2000, *The Legend of Wu Kong* and *Rose in the Wind*, published by the People's Literature Publishing House for the first time in April 2001 triggered off the second shock wave of cyber literature. Since then, Chinese cyber literature has made a dramatic leap towards commercialization, desirability, carnalization, and urbanization". Murong Xuecun's *Chengdu, Please Forget Me Tonight* is regarded as a "typical narrative of desire". The third wave of is represented by network works such as *Chengdu Fenzi*(Beautiful young girl)", *Shenzhen, Passionate Tonight*, *Chengdu, Love Only Eight Months*, *Heaven to the Left, Shenzhen to the Right*, etc. At this time, Chinese cyber literature is rapidly changing from free writing and amateur writing to commercialized writing and professional writing, and "it is rapidly changing from a kind of folk spontaneous literary behavior, new folk literature, and niche culture to the popular culture under the situation of commercial intervention and capital operation". Chen Cun thinks that "the best time for cyber literature has passed", but Ouyang Youquan obviously does not agree with him, instead, he thinks that "the pattern of cyber literature has become increasingly diversified and complicated, which is of positive significance to the maturity and healthy development of cyber literature" [1]. Ouyang Youquan's phasing method is more accurate in finding phasing nodes and has a better grasp of the characteristics of each period, but the specific scope of phasing is not given.

---

1 Ouyang Youquan, Introduction to Network Literature, Peking University Press, 2008, pp. 32-33.

Gao Xiaohui, in his article "Survey on the Current Situation of Cyber Literature", categorizes network literature into four phases as follows: the "start-up phase" in 1996-1997, the "first boom" in 1998-1999, the "harvest season" in 2000-2002 and the "growth in the doldrums" in 2003-2004.[1] Some researchers classify this process as "the budding period (1995-1996)", "Development (1997-1998)", "first Boom (1999-2000)," "trough period (2001-2002)", "second Boom (2003-2005)", "Stable Development Period (2006-present)." [2] Compared with Ouyang Youquan's phasing, these two phasing methods are more specific, but the criteria are vague and too trivial.

Yang Jianhong divided the development period of Internet literature into three stages: the "emerging period" (1991-1997), the "initial boom period" (1998-2002) and the "consolidation period" (2003-present). In the "Emergence Period", he defined the birth of Chinese cyber literature as 1991. In his view, the launching of the world's first weekly Chinese electronic magazine, Huaxia Digest, on April 5, 1991, is the source of Chinese cyber literature. The arrival of the "initial period" was marked by the popularity of Pizi Cai's The First Intimate Contact on the Internet in 1998. During this period, "representative works and writers emerged in large quantities", "traditional literature and traditional writers swirled into the cyber world", "columns and websites featuring original works on the net appeared competitively", and "the concept of cyber literature became popular"," "Internet literature competitions continue to be organized", "Capital operation has entered the Chinese language cyber literature".

---

1 Wang Xianji, edited by Wang Xianji, Survey Report on Certain Situations of Literary Creation since the New Century, Chunfeng Literary Publishing House, 2006, pp. 180-182.

2 Wang Xiaoying and Zhu Dong, "Looking Back and Reviewing: Ten Years of Internet Literature Research", Shanxi Normal University Journal (Social Science Edition), No. 2, 2010.

Murong Xuecun's Chengdu, Please Forget Me Tonight is regarded as a sign of the "period of consolidation". Cyber literature in this period also presented new features, such as "utilitarianism inhibited the deepening development of Internet creation", "blogging literature led to the broadening and dispersal of the horizons of Internet literature", "the collective transformation of representative Internet writers led Internet literature towards embarrassment", "The anti-conventional clamor of unconventional writers is highly criticized", "Post-80s writers have become the protagonists of web literature amidst the controversy", and so on.[1]

If we analyze the above phasing methods, we will find that not only do they divide the period into different periods, but they also divide the period into different nodes. For example, when was the beginning of Cyber literature in China? Ouyang Youquan did not mention it explicitly, and the following scholars have their own ideas, such as 1991, 1995, 1996, which really makes people feel at a loss as to where to start. In our opinion, this has something to do with the concepts they used, for example, Yang Jianhong used the concept of "Chinese language cyber literature", Gao Xiaohui used "Chinese cyber literature", and in Ouyang Youquan's case, it was "Mainland network literature", while other scholars used the term "cyber literature". A different concept will naturally define a different period of time. On the other hand, it is also related to the scholars' grasp of the development process of network literature. Even if we count from 1991, it is not more than twenty-one years since the development of Chinese cyber literature, but the amount of information in cyber literature is too large, and it is also updated and developed very rapidly. Compared with the rapid development of cyber literature, the research of academics is obviously lagging behind. Within a short period of time, the current academic community's research on online literature is still

1 Yang Jianhong, "The Staging of Chinese Network Literature", Journal of Henan Normal University (Philosophy and Social Science Edition), No. 4, 2009.

in its exploratory stage, and it is only natural that scholars have some differences in their views on the development stages of online literature.

In order to have a more authoritative and widely accepted staging of the development history of Internet literature in academic and cultural circles, there are at least three things that scholars should consider. First of all, is it Chinese cyber literature, Cyber literature of China or mainland cyber literature that we are staging? If this is not clearly defined, it is impossible to reach a unanimous opinion on the staging of the development of Cyber literature. Secondly, it is necessary to have a clearer grasp and explanation of the development of Chinese cyber literature over the past twenty years. When staging the works, it is necessary to explain the reasons for such a staging, and to list the representative literary works that support the staging. Otherwise, the work of staging will not be convincing. For example, in the current staging of Chinese cyber literature, *The First Intimate Contact* and *Chengdu, Please Forget Me Tonight* are relatively easy to be recognized as important demarcation points in the staging, because these two works are more representative, the former making the cyber literature as a form of creativity gradually become familiar to readers on the mainland, and the latter representing the advent of the professionalization and commercialization of online creativity. Thirdly, a "classicization" of online literary works in the past two decades is necessary. Although this approach may be criticized by many writers and critics of online literature, who think that the so-called "classicization" is contrary to the postmodernist spirit of cyber literature. However, the development of literary history has repeatedly demonstrated that without efforts to establish "canonization," it is extremely difficult for a period of literary history to be clearly defined and recognized by academia and society. [1]

---

1 In fact, the "classicization" of cyber literature has already been carried out quietly. For example, Lin Suer selected and edited the annual series of "Selected Chinese Internet Literature", and Banyan Tree Book Studio selected and edited the series of "China's Best Internet Literature of the Year". Although they may have selected these works out

What makes me me? - Characteristics of Cyber Literature

The reason why cyber literature is called cyber literature is that it must have its own characteristics that distinguish it from traditional literature. Otherwise, it is impossible to prove the reasonableness of its existence. Therefore, scholars who hold a positive attitude towards cyber literature have written articles to discuss the characteristics of cyber literature.

In recent years, there have been nearly 20 papers on the topic of "characteristics of Internet literature", and it is difficult to count the number of papers that partly talk about the characteristics of Internet literature. However, if we summarize the characteristics of network literature summarized in these articles,[1] we can find that the characteristics of cyber literature are mainly embodied in the following aspects:

1. The main body of creators is non-professionalized (civilianized), young and anonymous.

2. In terms of creative concept, it is manifested as the pursuit of entertainment and recreation, and the discharge of personal feelings; the aesthetic

of commercial interests, the positive significance of such work for the "classicization" of Internet literature should not be overlooked.

1 When summarizing the characteristics of online literature, the primary references include: Ke Xiujing, "The Aesthetic Characteristics of Online Literature" (Journal of South China Normal University (Social Sciences Edition), Issue 5, 2003), Sun Yijun and Gui Guomin, "On the Characteristics of Online Literature Creation in China" (Journal of Beijing University of Technology (Social Sciences Edition), 2003, Issue 5), Zhao Yonghong, "A Preliminary Discussion on Online Literature" (Journal of Inner Mongolia Normal University (Philosophy and Social Sciences Edition), 2004, Issue 4), Huang Laiming, "On the 'Textual' Characteristics of Online Literature" (Journal of Donghua University of Science and Technology (Social Sciences Edition), Vol. 4, 2004), Yu Minghua, "The Characteristics and Influence of Online Literature" (Journal of Hunan University of Humanities and Science, Vol. 3, 2005), Chen Ninglai, "On the Special Aesthetic Characteristics and Aesthetic Defects of Online Literature" (Journal of Qiqihar University (Philosophy and Social Sciences Edition), Vol. 1, 2007), An Wenjun, "Postmodernism and Online Literature" (Lanzhou Academic Journal, No. 11, 2008), Wang Sheng, "On the Openness of Online Literature" (Journal of Southwest Jiaotong University (Social Sciences Edition), Vol. 5, 2011), etc..

mentality is flattering and flattering, and the aesthetic orientation is depressed and decadent.

3. In terms of the creative process (method), it features decentralized freedom, flat game-like elements, interactive aesthetic approaches, rapidity, and openness.

4. In terms of creative content, the subject matter of creation is generalized, the main theme is marginalized, and the aesthetic content reflects the life of Internet users, their personal feelings and the true nature of life.

5. In the form of text, it pays attention to the hyperlinks of text and the technicality of multimedia, the openness of text, the intertextuality of network copying, the diversification of expression forms, the diversification of aesthetic symbols, the shortness of genre, and the simplicity and humor of language.

6. In terms of dissemination (reception), it manifests itself in the ecstasy of commercial consumption, the interactivity of reading, and the multi-dimensional aesthetic perspective of art appreciation.

The above is only a brief summary of our research in this area in recent years. From this summary, we can still see that there is more sense and less theoretical refinement in summarizing the characteristics of cyber literature. If we read these articles carefully, we will also find that there are a lot of repetitions and not enough innovations.

In the textbook Introduction to Cyber Literature published in 2008, Ouyang Youquan and others summarize the characteristics of cyber literature more concisely and deeply into the spirit of "New Folk Literature", the freedom of the virtual world, and the logic of post-modern culture. With regard to the spirit of "New Folk Literature", writers believe that it is mainly reflected in the linguistic orientation of "I write with my own hands", the popularized literary space, the narrative style of "profanity shows" and their spirit of resisting the sublime.

The freedom of the virtual world is mainly due to the fact that "the network equips the engine of freedom for literature", and the operation of network literature has a freer mechanism. Many scholars have seen the postmodern nature of Internet literature, but Ouyang Youquan and his colleagues have further organized this postmodern nature and made it more academic. For example, "the subversion of historical rationality", "the leveling of the depth mode", "opposition to authoritarianism, rejection of the center of the discourse", "the fragmentation of the subject", "the disappearance of the sense of distance", and so on. This kind of generalization and induction is obviously more scholastic.

Dare to ask where the road is? - The Development Trend of Internet Literature and Its Problems

In the course of the development of a new thing, there are always many problems, and this is also the case with online literature. The problems in the creation of cyber literature have become more prominent due to the late birth of cyber literature, the varying standards of its creators, and the difficulty in guiding and regulating it due to the characteristics of its online dissemination. Under such a situation, where will cyber literature go? How to guide the healthy development of cyber literature? This cannot help but attract the attention of scholars who are concerned about the development of network literature.

To summarize, we believe that the following problems exist in the development of online literature:

1. Low artistic quality. This state of affairs makes people only see "network" but not "literature", or only "literature" but not "literacy".

The main reasons for such a situation are: the dissipation of subjective consciousness, the loss of the spirit of creativity;[1] the low artistic cultivation of creators; [2]the serious phenomena of collage and imitation in the process of creation[3], and the negative influence of commercialization.

2. Serious dependence on technology. The Internet is only a technology, while literature originates from the spirit of mankind. Technology is only a tool borrowed in the process of literary creation, which should serve the purpose of literary creation and should not be used as a kind of capital for Internet literature to show itself off. As a matter of fact, such a problem does exist to a different extent in our cyber literature. "Due to the reliance on technology, the transcendence of aesthetic spirit by technical rationality in cyber literature has gradually led to the loss of elegant artistic flavor; the cyber space in cyber literature makes it possible for us to lose not only the connection between man and nature, but also the connection between man and the inner world ". [4]This has a very serious impact not only on literary creation but also on the spiritual existence of human beings.

3. Lack of commitment. The Internet is a virtual world and a free space. Here, people have removed the social veil of real life, and can be free of any constraints to express themselves.

It undoubtedly provides a possibility for literature to return to innocence. However, it also provides the possibility for internet writers to abuse their freedom, expand their personality and create inappropriate works. Due to the lack of a sense of responsibility, cyber literature may lose its sense of social

---

1 Chen Jiading, "A Few Faults of Network 'Hypertextual' Writing", Journal of Northwest Normal University (Social Science Edition), No. 6, 2009.
2 Yang Jianbing, "Can Everyone Become a Writer? - Questioning the Identity of Network Writers", Literary Review, No. 3, 2007.
3 Ma Jianmei, "Experimenting on the Guidance of Cyber Literature", Journal of Southwest National University (Humanities and Social Sciences Edition), No. 3, 2011.
4 Chen Jiading, "A Few Faults of 'Hypertextual' Writing on the Internet", Northwest Normal University Journal (Social Science Edition), No. 6, 2009.

responsibility, and may also lead to confusion about value standards. In this way, cyber literature will not only gradually drift away from our literature in terms of aesthetics, but also gradually lead itself astray in terms of social value.

4. Adverse effects of commercialization. We must admit that under the condition of a market economy, not only is Cyber literature affected by commercialization, but also traditional literature. Under this situation, the commercialization of Internet literature is inevitable, and commercialization has also promoted the development of cyber literature to a certain extent. However, literature is not a pure commodity after all. It is something belonging to the human soul. The commercialization of literature should be confined within reasonable limits. "But today's cyber literature, under the continuous corrosion of commercialization, has become a gold mine for writer, website, investors. For Internet companies, the profit model has become the most important thing."[1] In the bad influence of commercialization, in order to pursue the buy point, get more profits, network writers are desperately pandering to the readers. As a result, Mu Zimei's "body writing", ZhuYingQingTong's "sex articles", Rascal Yan's "nude photos" and other incidents have repeatedly caused a climax in online literature. As a result, cyber literature began to pursue the ease and pleasure of the physical senses, escaping from the majestic and tragic epic style, and such cyber literature has slowly become only visual impact and sensory stimulation, and slowly there is no more depth of thought and aesthetic pursuit in it. This kind of commercialization may only bring Internet literature to extinction in the end.

The academic community has also recognized such shortcomings. To address these problems, different parties have made a lot of efforts to guide

1 Wang Ying, "Problems and Reflections of Cyber Literature in the Market Era", Nanfang Literature Forum, No. 3, 2009.

online literature on a healthy path of development. On April 2, 2007, the first "Advanced Seminar for Online Writers" was held at the Shanghai Academy of Social Sciences. On March 20, 2008, the "2008 Summit Forum on the Development of Online Literature" and the selection and signing of cooperative websites for the 2007 National Research Project - Annual Survey Report on National Literature Websites were held in Beijing. The purpose of the event was to build bridges so that people of traditional literature could understand cyber literature, people of cyber literature could make their voices heard, and people of traditional literature could understand what literary websites were doing. On December 4, 2008, the Chinese Academy of Social Sciences held the second High-level Forum on Media Culture and Cyber Literature. On June 15, 2009, Literature Newspaper and Shanda Literature co-hosted a seminar on the works of the four writers from the starting point, and on July 15, 2009, the Lu Xun Academy of Literature held the first training class for writers of cyber literature. There are many other activities of this kind, and their purpose is quite obvious: to improve the artistic cultivation of cyber literature writers and to guide cyber literature towards a healthy development path. However, how useful is such "guidance" in the end? It is really hard to say, as some scholars have pointed out: "Successful online writers could not be 'guided'. [1] Mother and son or enemies? - Internet Literature and Traditional Literature

Since the birth of cyber literature, there have been endless thoughts and discussions on the relationship between cyber literature and traditional literature. This is because it is not only related to the development of cyber literature itself, but also to the re-division of the literary map of contemporary

1 Ma Jianmei, "Experimenting on the "Guidance" of Internet Literature", Journal of Southwest National University (Humanities and Social Sciences Edition), No. 3, 2011.

China, and even to the change and adjustment of the way of literary criticism and literary theoretical thinking.

The influence of cyber literature on traditional literature is basically closely related to the characteristics of cyber literature itself. Since the characteristics of cyber literature are summarized in the comparison between cyber literature and traditional literature, these new features will inevitably bring about certain impacts on traditional literature. Some scholars have pointed out that cyber literature has brought unique aesthetic styles and new literary concepts. There are three aspects of aesthetic changes: the development of sensualized aesthetics, the emergence of technologized aesthetics, and the convergence of Eastern and Western aesthetics; while new literary concepts are reflected in the gradual emergence of "macroliterature" and "quasi-literature", and "popularization" view of literature[1]. Some scholars take blogging literature as an example to elaborate on the impact of cyber literature on traditional literature. He thinks that the change of the main body of cyber literature has broken the monopoly of elite intellectuals on literary creation, the aesthetic pursuit of spiritual ecstasy has broken the traditional value concept of literature, which emphasizes on education, and the change of creative space, creative method and publication process has changed the production mode of traditional literature.[2] Some scholars have discussed the contribution of cyber literature to Chinese literature from the perspective of literary development, They argued that cyber literature has brought the prosperity of popular literature, changed the map of contemporary literature, impacted the literary system, truly realized the prosperity of literature in the public, provided fresh writing experience, and gained vitality for the

---

1 Yang Tuo: "Unique Aesthetics and New Literary Outlook - The Impact of Internet Literature", Jiangxi Social Sciences, No. 10, 2008.

2 Chen Dengbao: "On the Impact of Blog Literature on Traditional Literature", Zhongzhou Xuejian, No. 4, 2008.

diversified development of contemporary literature.[1] There are also scholars who describe the duel between cyber literature and paper-based literature, and believe that cyber literature has become the most energetic landscape of the literary scene, while paper-based literature is cold and bleak. In spite of this, paper-based literature will not give up its literary orientation voluntarily. Therefore, we should cross the boundary between paper media and online media, and seek the possibility of integrating paper literature with online literature. [2]

Summarizing the discussions of scholars on this issue, we find that they basically hold a positive attitude towards the impact and influence of cyber literature on contemporary literature, believing that such an influence will bring about certain changes in the literary landscape and literary concepts, which is conducive to the healthy development of literature. However, we all see clearly the problems of cyber literature, and we are not willing to give up the excellent traditions of traditional literature. Therefore, the search for the harmonious development of cyber literature and traditional literature has become the direction of scholars' efforts. As some scholars concluded, "Since its birth in the 1990s, cyber literature has made positive contributions to the promotion of literary return, the popularization of literature and the formation of literary feedback mechanisms. At the same time, cyber literature also has many contradictions such as aesthetic and non-aesthetic, utilitarian and non-utilitarian. We expect cyber literature to face the contradictions, solve the problems, establish a harmonious relationship with traditional literature with mutual learning and complementarity, coexistence and co-prosperity, and

---

1 Zhou Zhixiong: "Internet Literature and the Development of Contemporary Chinese Literature", Journal of Theory, No.4, 2009.

2 Tian Zhonghui, "Opposition and Integration: A Brief Discussion on the Interaction between Paper Literature and Internet Literature: Taking the Background of Post-80s and Post-90s Reading Groups", Literature and Arts Controversy, No. 8, 2010.

play a greater role in the construction of a harmonious culture in the new era". 1

What Can I Do to Save You? - Rethinking Cyber Literature Research

Basically, the research on cyber literature has been in step with the production of cyber literature, and has already passed through more than ten years. However, if we do a comprehensive reflection on these ten years of research, we will find that there are still a lot of unsatisfactory aspects. The problems are mainly reflected in the following aspects:

Firstly, mainstream scholars and mainstream academic journals have not paid enough attention to the study of cyber literature. Although this article has listed some "examples" at the beginning of this article that cyber literature has become the hot spot of contemporary literature research. However, those data can only prove that the research on Internet literature has a relatively lively atmosphere in the current academic landscape, and the factors behind this lively atmosphere have to be further analyzed. In fact, if we compare the study of cyber literature with other academic topics in contemporary literature, we will soon find out to what extent the study of cyber literature has been neglected! First of all, let us compare cyber literary research with contemporary writers' case studies. On CNKI, we found 913 academic articles under the title of "Cyber Literature" and 2137 articles under the theme of "Cyber Literature"; In the same way, we obtained the data of 992/2946, 903/2204 and 923/1642 papers on Jia Ping'wa, Wang Anyi and Yu Hua respectively from 1991 to 2012. The academic papers researched in a specific discipline (such as the textbooks and classrooms of Central South University) are almost on par with the research papers of a writer during the same time

1 Deng Shizhong, "Pursuing the Harmonious Development of Network Literature and Traditional Literature - A Brief Discussion on the Status of Network Literature in the New Century", Journal of Southwest University for Nationalities (Humanities and Social Sciences Edition), No. 4, 2007.

period! This is also the result of the inclusion of all journals. If we were to count the papers published in mainstream academic journals in the field of contemporary literature research that are titled "cyber literature," "Jia Pingwa," "Wang Anyi," or "Yu Hua," the results would be even more embarrassing. For the convenience of description, we have formulated Table 1.

Table 1 Statistics on Internet Literature and Writings by Jia Pingwa and Other Writers

	Literature Criticism	Contemporary Writers' Comments	Fiction Criticism	Literature Controversy	South Literary Forum	Contemporary Literary Forum	Total (Pieces)
Cyber Literature	8	1	3	15	15	15	57
Jia Pingwa	10	40	53	15	5	33	156
Wang Anyi	8	41	28	9	2	29	117
Yu Hua	4	29	23	16	7	19	98

Through Table 1, we can find that in the mainstream academic journals of contemporary literature, there is still a big gap between the research on cyber literature and the case studies of contemporary famous writers.

We will now compare online literature studies with the currently popular "return to the 1980s" and "new century literature studies." Among the scholars of Internet literature, except for Ouyang Youquan, there are very few well-known scholars, and they are mainly young scholars who do not have the right to speak in the academic circle. There are many famous scholars engaged in the "Return to the 1980s" and "New Century Literature Studies". The scholars working on the "Return to the 1980s" are mainly concentrated in famous universities in Beijing and Shanghai, such as Cheng Guangwei and his doctoral students from Renmin University of China, Hong Zicheng, Li Yang and He Guimei from Peking University, and Cai Xiang from Shanghai University, etc. Although scholars involved in "New Century

Literature Research" are scattered, there are many famous scholars, such as Lei Da, Bai Ye, Yu Kejun, Meng Fanhua, Zhang Yiwu, Cheng Guangwei, Wang Guangdong, and so on. From this comparison, we can see that the focus of mainstream scholars is hardly on cyber literature.

Through the above two comparisons, we can know that the whole academic circle attaches far less importance to the research of cyber literature. Of course, we must admit that the quality of cyber literature itself affects to a certain extent the importance attached to it by academics, but it is also an indisputable fact that academics have paid little attention to the study of cyber literature.

Secondly, there is a serious gap between research and creation. To a certain extent, the cyber literature discussed by researchers is mostly a figment of their own imagination, which is far from the vivid nature of cyber literature. This situation is mainly reflected in the overly homogenous nature of the research object. In recent years, research on cyber literature has focused on a few limited works by a few limited writers such as Pizi Cai, Murong Xuecun, Annie Baby and Li Xunhuan, such as The First Intimate Contact, Chengdu, Forget Me Tonight, Heaven to the Left, Shenzhen to the Right, The Legend of Wu Kong, Farewell to Vivian, Chengdu Fenzi, Chengdu, Love in Eight Months, etc. The gap between research and creation is also reflected in the fact that many scholars apply the research mode of traditional literature to the research of cyber literature. Because these scholars do not know enough about cyber literature, or even lack the necessary knowledge of cyberspace and other new media, they have to adopt the traditional theoretical model in their research. This kind of research may be a kind of "aphasia", or give people the feeling of scratching the itch.

Thirdly, there are more repetitions of macro studies and less analysis of writers' works. If we do a preliminary statistical analysis of the research papers on cyber literature in the past ten years, we can find that there are very few textual analyses of specific writers and works. This is, on the one hand, related to the fact that the quality of cyber literature is generally low, and on the other hand, closely related to the fact that critics generally take cyber literature lightly. In the minds of many scholars, the study of cyber literature is not really academic research, and important scholars and critics seldom spend their energy on the textual interpretation of cyber literature. Even when they do conduct research on cyber literature, they often adopt a macro perspective to assess cyber literature as a whole,[1] focusing on the legal issues of cyber literature, the characteristics of cyber literature, the shortcomings of cyber literature creation, and other aspects that seem grand at first glance, but when we synthesize these articles, we will find that the phenomenon of repetition is quite serious. Fourthly, the research is superficial and lacks depth. The current criticism of online literature mainly manifests itself in the following types: insightful, entertaining, subversive, and attention-grabbing criticism, which clearly lacks theoretical analysis. Many research articles fashionably use postmodern theory, consumption theory and carnivalization theory, but not many of them really apply them appropriately; on the contrary, the phenomenon of copying and adapting them is frequently seen.

To sum up, cyber literature research has indeed made remarkable achievements in the new century, providing academic resources and research paths for the diversified development of contemporary literary research. However, at the same time, we should also see that the problems existing in cyber literature research are still very serious, and if these problems cannot be solved in future academic research, the idea of disciplining cyber literature research will only be an ideal.

Journal of Zhoukou Normal College, Issue 1, 2013

---

1 In Literary Review, Issue 5, 2011, we read an article by Mr. Wang Xiaoming, a famous scholar, entitled "Six Divisions of the World: Chinese Literature Today". The article analyzes the new literary landscape of today's China from a broad perspective, including an analysis of online literature. This article typically represents the mainstream scholars' approach to Internet literature in contemporary literary studies.

Afterwords

I have been looking forward to this collection for a long time. There are two reasons. First, I once thought that it would be my first published work; second, it is also one of the "Henan Critics Series". But, for reasons both imagined and unimagined, it has been delayed for so long!

In retrospect, it was probably in the spring that this collection came into being. I was waiting for the train at the high-speed railway station when Qiao Ye sent me a spreadsheet and asked me to fill it out. I had never published a book before, and I was so happy to be invited to join such a series of writings that you can imagine the joy. As requested, I quickly compiled a selection of articles that I thought were still presentable, decided on a title for the collection, and sent it to the publisher as soon as possible. From that moment on, my anticipation underwent many changes, but now it has settled into calm. Although the wait was long, the fact that it was finally published is something worth celebrating. I would like to thank Ms. Qiao Ye for giving me the opportunity to publish this collection, as well as Mr. Hou Ruoyu and Ms. Han Lu for their hard work on it. If this collection is a small tree, then it is Ms. Qiao Ye who provided the soil for it to grow, and it is Mr. Hou Ruoyu and Ms. Han Lu who continuously watered and fertilized it, so that it finally survived and thrived.

The title of the book "The Three Faces of Literary Criticism" is in fact a bit of a misnomer, at least the text in the second series of "Literary Studies of the Eighties" cannot be called "Literary Criticism", but it is vaguely named so in order to be consistent with the series of "Henan Critics". Although the title of the book is a bit far-fetched, the text basically reflects the direction of my research in organizing these texts: contemporary Henan literary criticism, the new century literary criticism, and studies on the literature of the 1980s. Up to now, the scope of my study has basically revolved around these three fields.

But this is not to say that I am so satisfied with my own research and with the words in this collection. Looking back now at the words I wrote back then, especially the critical pieces, I can't say I'm ashamed, but at least I feel a bit embarrassed: I lacked talent and had a limited perspective. Some of these were even published ten years ago, and reading them now, one can't help but feel that I was just squeezing out the last drops of creativity and reheating old ideas—a sign of a writer whose talent has dried up! Although some of my writings were painfully omitted due to length constraints and the early publication of this collection, and my recent research findings could not be included, it ultimately boils down to my own lack of talent and shallow knowledge—there simply isn't enough to choose from! But perhaps that's for the best; there wasn't much worth preserving in the first place, so why bother piecing together so much?

Finally, it should be reported that although the field of research has basically remained unchanged, the focus of efforts has changed somewhat. Between the study of literary history and literary criticism, the focus has been more on the study of literary history and less on literary criticism in recent years; between New Century Literature and Contemporary Henan Literature, the scope of attention has been more focused on the local area of Henan. This is evident in some of the projects that have been submitted and approved in the past few years. From the Henan Provincial Philosophy and Society Planning Project to the Ministry of Education Project to the National Social Science Project, the topics are all limited to the literary activities of modern Chinese writers in the 1980s. In the field of contemporary literature in Henan, the efforts of the last two years have been directed towards the compilation and publication of the "Chronicle Series of the Central Plains Writers Group".

We must not forget where we came from. No matter how long it takes, we should never forget the teachers who provided the opportunity to publish these articles. It is because of the opportunity and the hard work of the editors that my "academic achievements" have been finalized, and the initial path of my academic research has been laid down for me to hobble along. Thank you!

Xu Hongjun

May 1, 2023

This book was published as interim research results of the following project: Humanities and Social Sciences Research of the Ministry of Education in 2019 "Compilation and Research of Writers' Memories in the 1980s" (19YJC751052), 2020 Henan Province Higher Education Science and Technology Innovation Talent Support Program (Humanities and Social Sciences Category) "Compilation and Research of Historical Materials from the Memoirs of Modern Chinese Writers" (2020-cx-021), and 2022 National Social Science Fund Annual Project "Research on the Literary Creation of Modern Chinese Writers in the 1980s" (22BZW159).

www.ingramcontent.com/pod-product-compliance
Lightning Source LLC
LaVergne TN
LVHW010653110826
845149LV00014B/3073

* 9 7 8 1 9 6 5 8 9 0 9 3 6 *